HALLUCINATIONS FROM HELL

HALLUCINATIONS FROM HELL
CONFESSIONS OF AN ANGRY SAMOAN

GREGG H. TURNER

THIS IS A GENUINE RARE BIRD BOOK

Rare Bird Books
453 South Spring Street, Suite 302
Los Angeles, CA 90013
rarebirdbooks.com

Set in Warnock
Printed in the United States

Illustrations for Chapters 1, 2, 4, 5, 7, 9, 12, 15, 17, 18 by Gary Panter

Illustrations for Chapters 3, 6, 8, 10, 11, 13, 14, 16, 19 by Mindy Turner

Author photograph by Nate Duran

write Gregg: gregg@greggturner.com

10 9 8 7 6 5 4 3 2 1

Library of Congress Cataloging-in-Publication Data available upon request.

This book is dedicated to my pal, former bandmate, and legendary beat-scribe Richard Meltzer

Special thanks to my former *CREEM* editors Bill Holdship, John Kordosh, Billy Altman, and Dave DiMartino, as well as Gary Panter, Dave Lebow, and Mindy Turner, who provided the swell sketches for the stories.

Not forgetting the following folks who enabled these hallucinations over the years:

Ronn Spencer, Andy Shernoff, Phast Phred Patterson, Jennifer Stephens, Metal Mike Saunders, Todd "The Hippie Stabber" Homer, Billy Bill Miller, Brenna Sardina, Shannon Gilbert Bagent, Michelle Kozuchowski, Hank Jones, Jeff Gold, Steve Besser, Roky Erickson (RIP), and lots of other folks.

Gratitude to Tyson Cornell, Peter Heur, and Bruce Duff for making this happen.

Thank you to my editor, Dave DiMartino.

"It broke your father's heart
when you became an Angry Samoan..."

CONTENTS

EDITOR'S FOREWORD

I think it was the cup of pus. Yep, it was a cup of pus, from the story of the same name, that reminded me what kind of guy Gregg Turner was. And is.

He is the kind of guy who could lead a singular life—an enlightened music writer and fan, songwriter, musician, Angry Samoan, PhD, and actual, real-life, newly retired college professor, and father—and still take the time to construct, or recount, a world in which a cup of pus might very naturally be stored in someone's refrigerator. And in that same world, that same someone might or might not be housing a twenty-six-foot tapeworm in their innards. It is possible, if not plausible, but it is a part of the world that Gregg Turner delightfully inhabits and shares with us here.

The Gregg Turner perspective is unlike any other: he paints a vivid, believable picture of academia over here, of the obtuse snobberies to be had in the world of art galleries over there, and, smack in the middle of nowhere, the joys of exhibiting stuffed weasels on your toaster oven and TV—the latter, no less, in his compellingly titled tale "Maggots." That all of this comes from a man with an extensive knowledge of music—not just music, but *good* music—who is a onetime member of the storied VOM, a celebrated Angry Samoan, and a longtime believer in the mystic worth of the 13th Floor Elevators' Roky Erickson (*and* is his Horror Pal!)—makes it invaluable, fun, and unforgettably weird. In a good way.

I have known Gregg Turner since the seventies, working with him at CREEM and beyond. He never, ever let us down, he never, ever let *me* down, and the tales that follow will most assuredly lighten your load for the remainder of your natural years. Crème brûlée will never taste the same again!

Meet you at the Colonic Café.

Dave DiMartino
Los Angeles, 2021

AUTHOR'S FOREWORD

For anyone who has known me over the last few decades, I have this rap of blathering on forever with what are perceived to be improbable anecdotes and stories, typically overstaying my welcome. Well, to be honest, I get nervous around folks and I try to diffuse my discomfort by prattling on with crazy shit I've observed around me or misbegotten tales that I think will get a reaction. Hallucinations? The stories in this here anthology may in fact be true wild tales I've absorbed over time. Perhaps drenched with generous hyperbole? I'll let you decide. Friends have insisted I translate these hallucinatory depictions of fragile reality to text. So over the long haul, I've documented these accounts and transcribed in marginal space on computers and scraps of dog-eared paper since 1975.

Hey—I just retired from professing math at my university here in New Mexico where I was a tenured faculty member for decades. That means it's finally time to pay dues and actually collect these seamy stories and release as the compilation you currently hold in your paws. Hence, I will be spared future necessity of ambushing this spiel on unwitting victims—I can now just throw this tome up in the air and hope it sticks. Somewhere.

I am well known for my "Tapeworm Story," which is a rather gnarly freak-out involving some poor fuck who gestated a gigantic parasite long after an all-night sushi binge. This was handed down to me from a friend whose dad actually doctored the dude! The narrative presented here is primarily a transcript of a protracted chat with two acquaintances—a former student ("Sarah") and a Slovakian computer science colleague (let's call him "Artov"). Their reactions to the details are almost as sour as the tale itself. It's pretty harebrained and, to separate fact from hallucinations, I corroborated the logistics, at the time, from the doctor firsthand. There were times, I confess, when students in my after-lunch Calculus class, collectively closing eyes from one of my inspired lectures, begged diversion. I would ask if they'd prefer to hear the Tapeworm Story. "YEAH, YEAH," they would bleat, and without waiting for extra encouragement, I'd jump into it. Frequently a few would excuse themselves to the lavatory halfway through, presumably the PB&J they had devoured for lunch threatening expulsion.

In fact, more than a handful of these "Hallucinations from Hell" lean on the bilious side of the street ("Maggots," "A Cup of Pus," etc.) but transcription of the repulsive is not the intended theme of this book. Whether it's about mathematical nightmare ("Twenty Fig Newtons") or of pest-ridders from the dark side ("AOK Pest Control"), these tales chronicle a not-so-distant dimension of life on this planet. Really, I'm more of a voyeur and journalistic muse processing this unlikely reality as it constricts my first-witness belly like a pissed-off python snake.

And the Roky Erickson yarns (Roky, some of you might know, was the lead singer-songwriter of Texas 1960s psychedelic cult band, the 13th Floor Elevators) are totally legit. He was a colorful guy back in the time (boy, could he write amazing, riveting tunes! And that voice!). Eventually Roky emerged as a legendary performer and well-followed musical icon thirty years later, albeit less with the stream of conscious Luciferian fountain of froth that he maniacally expelled back in 1978. Did the killer bees really swarm his motel room and instigate a "brain hernia" that nearly prevented his performance at the Whisky a Go Go the next night? Yup. I was there. If you don't believe me, ask the Aliens' (Roky's backing band) electric autoharp sorcerer Billy Bill Miller. He was there too!

The Roky story in this book harps on the queer and transcendent mental wavelength he dialed back in those days. He'd always tell me we were "horror pals!" (an accolade I to this day hold close to my heart). But I'm not in any way, shape, or form using this documentation of bizarre behavior to make fun of the guy. His talents have been incredibly inspirational—his improbable appearance with Doug Sahm at the Palomino Club in North Hollywood in 1975 was a game changer for me. I was hypnotized—the authority of his voice and larger-than-life performance that night turned everything upside down. The redneck, beer-swilling, steak-chomping cowboys in the audience, presumably there for good ol' boy Sir Doug's tunes, aspirated their steak sauce when Roky, called onstage in Sahm's last set, started wailing like a two-headed dog!

Speaking of dogs, "No More Dog" tells the sad story of a mad hound hunt gone bad. It centers around this retro rockabilly dude "Hank Jones" and his affection for pooches and women. Some of you may know him. Hank is a dear friend of mine, a kind soul, and a very talented, unusually intelligent and sensitive musician and singer-songwriter. In this particular version of canine lust, I have employed a measure of extravagance to paint some unseemly behavior and klutziness. This is to keep you, the reader, entertained! The germ (and related germs) of this epic tale leans heavily on the non-fictional side—it happened, I'm tellin' ya—but here I allow for some compassionate—uhm, okay I'll say it—exaggeration. Hopefully Jones will dig this and not wanna kill me.

The names have been changed to protect the innocent in most of these here hallucinatory accounts. Any semblance of congruency to humanoids you might know is mere coincidence. You may or may not recognize the "Sheep Eaters" as a familiar punk-rock combo of some brief notoriety. "Open Mic" was sourced from a real open mic night circus I witnessed in Harvard Square when I (unfortunately) had to spend a year in Worse-ter, Massachusetts, back in 1999 (frequent trips to Boston and Providence were demanded 'cause Worcester is an abysmal hellhole, though Abbie Hoffman hailed from the place). I took copious notes that evening. The whole operation was a shameful scam. The performers each were asked to pay ten bucks to do their thing. Boo.

And in 1996 Santa Fe, I created and hosted a one-hour weekly AM-dial Sunday afternoon radio show attempting to capture local nut bones offering their life twists live on the air (no shortage of lid flippers here in Santa Fe, New Mexico). Commonly these got out of hand and the station manager, if he tuned in, would pop an aneurism. Like the time we had fetish bondage practitioners lay out "proper slave spanking technique" (forty-five degrees to the butt plane, we're told) or when an alien abductee from Roswell confessed she was the beneficiary of an alien-induced orgasm in the saucer's command room. She said they used an "alien garden hose." Whatever.

TRUTH BE TOLD! You don't believe me? More hallucinations? Check out testimony from my psychiatrist, who will argue that my veracity has not been compromised by psychotic delusion! And my most talented math student from Pitzer College will vouch for the onslaught of classroom tales that mixed with the lessons back in 1987. So I have cred to back me up!

In the prescient words of the old man holding court in "The Poet,"
"Blood, bath, love, have
Not forgotten in the moonlight
Shower, shower, water falling all over
Now's it's time…and the time is right!"

I have no clue what this means—but that's what he said at 3:00 a.m. in Venice Beach upstairs at the *Van Gogh's Ear* all-night coffee dump. I wrote it down. Honest. *"Now it's time...and the time is right!"* Indeed.

Gregg H. Turner
Santa Fe, New Mexico
Post-Trump, 2021

THE POET
MARCH 1992

The old guy was the center of attention. His gray receding hair was pulled back in a short, stubby ponytail. He had a 'stache and a two-thirds goat, both of these gray and black, and he was sitting upright at the largest Goodwill-quality table of tired oak to be found here in this upstairs coffee dump.

Not too crowded at two or three in the morning and the newly spawned twenty-four-hour hangout, been open just a few weeks, was already gaining a late-night clique of weathered neophyte hippies, homeless surfers, assorted over-the-counter drug fiends, Harley dudes, cosmic fortune tellers, close-cousin metaphysical hobos, curious yuppies, and caffeine-addled insomniacs. The sister operation on the beach had not been able to turn a profit due to chronic infestation of an even *slimier* group—fascist beach bums and other related sub-species of humanoid dreck which, along with the kelp and sand crabs, apparently wound up at this establishment's front door with painful regularity. Location number one on the sand was the model the owners of number two wished to avoid. Nevertheless, things have a way of restoring equilibrium, a homeostasis of freak allure which seems to beckon and insect-trail the insects out from their nighttime stealth. And so, despite the intention to attract an upscale version of life (and profit), a transplanted mass of all-too-familiar downscale versions quickly found their way over, massed and anxious, planted in the invisible evening shadows like a horde of hungry cockroaches roosted beneath the paneled walls of a grimy Thai food mall stop.

Upstairs, perched regal and way upright on a tall wooden highchair, The Poet looked like a worn-out blend of Salvador Dalí and the old martial arts guy in *Karate Kid*. Only possibly appropriate in Venice Beach, which is where we were that night, and where we would be for many other nights because we lived across the street and usually produced our best results (technical research notes) in noisy, grungy, rodent-laden hellholes. That is to say, plus or minus the vermin, our across-the-street clubhouse possessed all the earmarks of quality office space.

They assembled at the long table near the side wall. The Poet had, as far as I could make out, twelve—let's call them "disciples"—unkempt hairy teenagers and a couple scruffy girls, apparently earnest in rapt attention to each syllable and consonant he expelled. I could not...make out the words, but it seemed like...some kind of...game (could it be?)...was goin' on. I craned my neck toward the banter, just to catch the vibe—what could this dude be dispensing, what kind of psychic Band-Aids could he offer to possibly splint the rupture of this random sample of wasted minds?

"*Disease*," the girl proclaimed loudly, and all eyes turned on the Poet.

He acknowledged the entry, furrowed his brow, then triumphantly responded: "Seven. Disease is a seven."

They all nodded eagerly. Then, counterclockwise, the next solemn face broke equally solemn eye contact with the floor and engaged the countenance of the old man. "*Oxygen*," he finally offered. "*Oxygen*."

Not caught off guard, the Poet nodded and embraced this at once. Perhaps it should've come up earlier. "Well, we certainly need it," he mused. "Okay, six, oh, well, say six and a half. Oxygen is six and a half." Several of the seated sycophants felt that a seven might've been more in line, disappointed, but they said nothing. And the game continued.

But was it a game? A contest? A Ritual? Some crazy group therapy? I had...never...witnessed anything...quite like this. I could no longer transcribe my own equations. Upper bounds of moduli of analytic functions suddenly withered in importance and, more than compulsively transfixed, I waited for another...uh, category.

"*ANGER!*," shouted the next disciple. He wasn't angry, but certainly emphatic.

"Anger is between four and five. Calm down."

"*Logic*," screamed another.

"Nine! Logic is always nine."

"*The earthquakes.*"

"I say eight and a half, eight and a half for an earthquake."

"No, *plural*," corrected the one who offered the topic. "I mean the earth*quakes*, *all* of them," he insisted.

"*Collectively*, then? Well, I suppose it makes more sense to group them together. But you have to understand that as a collection, they diminish their significance. Do you understand this, are you clear about my point? And in this case, I'll have to say the earthquakes are seven. Seven for them all, no more. No arguments about this either. I'm strong on the point."

There appeared to be little dissent, and a snub-nosed kid with half a beard jumped in quickly: "*Pain.*"

"Pain is seven, Suffering is nine."

"*Zoo*," shouted a girl with some darkish schmutz on her forehead. "Zoo."

"Two. Two for the Zoo." They kept going; all of the Poet's disciples continued to chime in.

"*Remorse.*"

"Eight—yes: eight for remorse, but tomorrow it could be nine and a half."

"The Accountant," blurted a teen wearing his high school colors and an LA Dodgers baseball cap.

"Uhhhm, yes, I remember. This came up last week."

"But we tabled it," reminded one of the others, some washed-up house painter who had earlier passed around business cards soliciting gigs as the group first assembled. "You promised to consider it tonight, as unfinished business."

"Did I?" The old guy tugged at the deft tuft of fur on his chin. "Let's say this," he pondered. "The accountant is concise, the accountant must also be *pre*cise—thus, he is twicely *cise*. So for that, let's wrap it up, give the accountant at least a six, and that's being generous. But having said all of that, I don't ever want to hear of the accountant again, is that understood?" He seemed to break his stride here for a second, tugged at his tuft again, and remarked that "it's an over *over*rated profession," to which the tenth grader (?) who threw out the topic for evaluation, blurted, "Yeah, tell me about it, my old man's a fuckin' money merchant, and he's a worthless, boring piece o' shit. He never plays basketball with me on our driveway in front of the house and all his fuckin' silk ties, they're all the same fuckin' color, man."

"Well, I'm sorry about that, but then again…I'm really not sorry at all. What do you expect?"

The kid blurted out, "I don't expect nothin', I've *never* expected nothin'…I just turned sixteen," but the thought was quickly truncated.

The Poet, as a rule, discouraged such banter. He seemed uncomfortable with this type of discourse as it drifted from the ratings; he dismissed the kid's qualification with a flip wave of the hand, and to the accountant's son he suddenly snarled, "*Just shut up, that's enough out of you.*" He seemed to hiss, and then alluded to the fact that he was no longer enjoying himself, the topics tonight disappointed him, that the group needed to retrieve the "focus" that

Gregg Turner

was there the previous week. A young woman raised her hand and introduced herself as "Lacey" (to which the old man shot back with "I don't care *what* your name is, but if you ever waste time identifying yourself in this way again, I will call you Lucille; we will all call you Lucille"); she wondered if any of the ratings could be reconsidered.

Or "Are they final?"

The Poet told her to "shut her trap," that she talks "too much," but he responded by pointing at the long-haired, hippie-ish guy next to her, rhetorically asking, "Can the numbers be changed?"

The hairy kid shook his mane and reported dutifully that all results are "totally final, man."

This pleased the Poet. He nodded with a smile and said "yesssssssssss—get it?"

They all nodded in accordance, then a gaping silence. Now, they looked at The Last Disciple, the one who had been quiet. She was younger, not legally an adult. Sullen and pretty, but with big ears. She'd prefer to watch and not say anything. But the old man would not let her pass. With a suddenly penetrating glance, the Poet invoked the youngster who then timidly engaged the opportunity. Turning to the old man, she whispered, and whispered quite clearly so we all could hear: "*Love...*" Then again, louder and this time more certain: "*LOVE.*"

The old guy stuffed a piece of bread in his mouth, and his jaws worked with extra pressure, meticulously masticating on what the proper modality would be for rating this. And he muttered something I couldn't fully pick up, and asked if they really wanted to go there. He clasped his hands together and bowed his head to meditate on the gravity of the pronouncement he was about to confer. I mean, there was gravity for sure—the silence as he deliberated was not vacuous; his sudden concentration appeared to be pregnant with a poignancy that was distinct from the earlier ritual. From my angle of observation in the corner of the room, riveted to this whole crazy circus, I counted countenances. I could spot the looks of inevitability, of those who were clear that the topic now would recruit his attention. Had it been issued at a previous gathering? Deferred or "tabled" for some reason?

I can't tell you why, but I could very wildly dig something implicit in the air, that this had in fact come up many times before. This was confirmed when he looked up wearily, nodded his head, and said, "I know this is why you're here tonight, that this means a lot to you and I've promised before that we'd at least begin to broach the subject... but...well, I'm ready, I must say, to now jump beyond broach. I do care deeply about all of you and, after all, that's why we're here in the first place, why we've been together for the last several months; we're *all* certainly looking for answers. And so perhaps it's now time to take the leap. Maybe you're ready." He knew they wanted something large, something, say, above an eight. But there were many reasons that couldn't happen. Perhaps the easiest recourse would have been to allow rating inflation and keep everyone content. "*Content*," itself, had been given a two last month, had it not? Yes, this was the case. And "*moths*" was awarded an astounding nine. These kids knew what they were getting into when they came aboard, too late to turn back now. Time to break the bad news.

"Look," he started plaintively. "I'm not your mommies and daddies. I'm not here to sugarcoat this pissant world for you, you understand? You come to me for the truth. And if it breaks your spirit, well, so be it. Look at all of you. Your broken illusions and dreams are worn on your sleeves. The necrotic agony of living even the short, meager, often odious existence you've all somehow managed to accrue is quite obvious. Let me ask you, do you understand despair (six point five), do you appreciate heartache and the loneliness of the soul? DO YOU?"

They nodded in accordance. They seemed to understand, to get the old man's rap. I scrawled down on a napkin the diatribe. I wanted to remember it. I had no idea I'd be transcribing to explain or repeat to anyone else. He seemed to really care for these kids.

"Do you understand that we are each an uninhabited island, waiting for the cumulative infusion of carbon dioxide to bury our shore's sun-warmed sands? By meeting like this, we acknowledge our indignation of THE ENTIRE PROCESS—that life is a charade, it really means nothing. And that we shall accept nothing MORE than nothing as we wither into nothingness." Their mouths were open. He looked slowly at each one in turn. "Are you with me?"

Oh, yes, they were. A few stood up, pumping clenched fists. One hollered, "Okay, man, so GIVE IT TO US! Let us HAVE IT. We're so WITH you, man."

"Yeah," shouted another, "that's what this is all about!"

Still further on down the table, someone else, red-faced now, stood up and screamed, "Hey, man, don't candy coat nothin'. We got your twist—down!"

Even the accountant's son was riveted, and he suddenly belted out, "My old man, he comes home after work and, y'know, he sits his fat ass down in the recliner and the only thing that counts after that is a couple of cheap brews and a fuckin' TV sitcom."

Now they were all off their chairs, shaking their fists, visibly aroused. And the young girl, still stoic, in a subdued but steady voice, projecting above the ruckus, looked straight at the Poet—and he returned her laser-like focus—and said, "SO TELL US ABOUT LOVE. WHAT'S IT WORTH, MAN?"

He looked at all of them carefully. They were hungry. They were alone. They breathed fire. They wanted the truth. Hungry for the Truth. And they were ready. I turned my napkin over and continued with the crazy notes.

"I must introduce my feelings about this, this...this topic," he demurred. "It is not like the others; it is not for everyone. And it cannot be rated in the same breath as all of the other categories disseminated tonight." The Poet inhaled the deeply cold, turgid night air that had seeped into the small room from between the panes of the windows. He studied the facade of the young teenage girl and then locked into the group's cumulative desperation. They implored him to rate; strident, they began to stomp their feet on the floor: "RATE LOVE, RATE LOVE, RATE LOVE." The coffee server who worked behind the counter downstairs was standing below, holding onto the banister, waiting for the punch line.

"Well, before I do," gasped the old man, "I have a poem. First, a poem. Appropriately, I'm going to call this 'Love Poem (The Deep End).'" A felt pen on two more napkins, I got it all, this was his Love Poem (caps emphasis mine):

> You ask for a rating.
> I ask for peace.
> You ask for forgiveness,
> But I don't see it.
>
> You ask for nothing;
> That's why you're here.
> Still, I give you everything,
> And that's why I'M here.
>
> Blood, bath, love, have
> Not forgotten in the moonlight.
> Shower, shower, water falling all over.
>
> Now it's time—time and time.

Finally, you are an adult, swimming in your parents' pool
It's not Heated and you are alone in the Deep End.
And you cry when the sun goes down, "Mommy, Mommy, oh, Mommy,"
Because you are aware of something floating beside you—in

Gregg Turner

the Deep End.

Is it a turd? Or something meaningful and warm and visceral?
Whichever it is, children, that's the LAST thing you wanna
grab hold of.

> *Blood, bath, love, have*
> *Not forgotten in the moonlight.*
> *Shower, shower, water falling all over.*
> *Now it's time—the time is right.*

He bowed his head. The stomping had ceased after the second line into his "Love Poem." Boy, the room was silent, and the old man, he was suddenly cultivating this predatory look, like a vulture eyeballing roadkill from tree height.

"Okay, well here it is, then. I assign the mathematical constant i for LOVE; i is not real, it is imaginary, and yes, it is the square root of -1. Love must be this non-real constant. I rate LOVE to be i."

The Poet stood up, his face was now red, and he too clenched his fist in the air. "Well, that's it! It's over, it's done."

I ran out of napkin space, but from memory, this is what happened next:

"YES," they shouted back approval, they were foaming, frothing and just ecstatic at this proclamation. Oh, they didn't call him the Poet for nothing. He's laid out some shrewd ratings before, but this, this i for Love, who woulda thunk?

Okay, at this juncture, you may reasonably doubt my credulity, my first-person witness to such madness; after all, I was not an affiliate of these serious searching souls. Just doing some honest work, only the journalist inside of me allowed lucid snapshot observation of this ceremony. I was at the opposite end of the room; the illumination that the one bright lamp cast over to my table allowed viable atoms of transparency. So I'd been vaporized in a modest anonymity in the room's night shadows, offering nothing at all to the circus that had unfolded. But I can tell you this, the casting of this *i*-rating washed this strange evening's canvas with a sourly ironic eyewitness. It was as if Kafka and Burroughs, holding hands, had pissed from the heavens, showering down the blueprint for some flipped-out new TV game show.

He stretched, then quickly, without ceremony, the Poet excused himself and retreated down the stairs, seemingly wrung out and beat. It wasn't clear whether he was taking off and this was the end of the festivities or it was just intermission. Still, the kids at the table refused to quit.

"*Foreign Policy*," one yelled out.

But the Poet wasn't around to hear it—and they waited, as if "*foreign policy*" might signal the old man to come back. But no sign of the Poet and "*foreign policy*" was not rated.

"*Shirley Temple Black*"

No rating [where'd he go?].

"*Myasthenia Gravis*."

No rating [was he gone?].

"*Penis*."

Unrated once again... The disciples looked confused, possibly frantic—still they persisted.

"*Jerry Mathers*." [nothing]

The tall guy, apparently the elder statesman of the group (he looked mid-twenties), stood up, now a bit perturbed. "Where'd he go?" He revolved to the chick—the one who proposed love; she was staring silently out the window. "What the fuck, didn't we say we'd steer clear of ANYTHING like that tonight? What—you expected a two this time? Where the hell is he?" He pivoted to the only other person in the room (besides me) not a part of their tribe. Now more impatient then PO'd, the tall disciple interrogated the man at the next table: "You there, with the fisherman's hat, you got any idea where he went?"

Gregg Turner

"Nope."

Then he strode toward the stairs, eyeballing the group still assembled at the table of giant oak, and said: "I'll check his spot down there."

He pointed down there, down the stairs; the kid who'd got two for his "zoo" suggested looking "in the bathroom by the kitchen—he likes to hang there when he's upset." [Was he upset?]

The order at the table was disintegrating, now just half the original constituency still seated. They did not appear to be agitated or even annoyed—just looking around, almost routinely bored. Downstairs, they checked the john, but no Poet. They yelled for someone to spy on his "favorite bush in the parking lot" where he sometimes urinates in the "lamp shadows behind empty parked cars." But apparently no fresh, discernible liquid waste was detected. Finally, two or three more get up to expand the search ["Why'd he take off so abruptly, man? This is screwed up, I was next, I was gonna ask him to rate 'great-grandfather'"].

"Nah, he's flown! He's a ghost."

"Maybe his pancreas was acting up again?"

"I don't fucking know." It seemed like the tall guy was way out of sorts now. "I think we should reassemble and wait. He might be coming back."

So they did this, fifteen or twenty minutes must've passed, but the old guy was, in fact, a history-book person. Still, they were sitting there, back at the table, collective frozen expressions of nothingness, still as mice. Each writing [notes? more topics just in case?]. Nothingness, ambient quiet. Opaque quiet. The bathroom door downstairs closed, opened, then slammed tight. Closed and opened once more. Closed again. A toilet flushed, the sink was being used. The water ran from the faucet full throttle. Three or four of those kids were running around, they were making all this commotion and noise. Like they were firing off signals, hoping he'd answer or respond.

But the old man was gone, he was gone, flown the coffee dump. Now it was clear that the strategy to beckon his return, beacon their desperation for his *uhmm* guidance, was to amplify his favorite bathroom sounds and to leave the sink running (this apparently worked once before)—but all o'this was failing miserably.

My train of thought broken, my impetus to finish whatever it was that brought me there in the first place long gone, I figured I'd had enough, so I walked down the stairs, emerged from below the neon facade of Van Gogh's Ear, and then (somewhat reluctantly) I hurried off across the street. It was half past four in the morning—and from the psychic safety of greater distance, halfway across the boulevard right on the yellow center stripe, the midpoint point of the sand-blown asphalt, I discerned...what sounded like...the reemergence of a Poet-less group. Their voices were more strident, perhaps suddenly aggressive. Was this one final construction to gain his presence [from behind the bushes]? They continued. I could hear them easily out there in the street through the cracked window on the second floor above the oak table. But the topics now issued sounded plaintive, wounded, and peculiarly hollow.

"*Drones,*" one of them brayed painfully.

"*Chemical Fallout.*"

"*Proof through the night.*"

[no response, no rating]

The tall guy at the table forced the window further ajar above the table where they were still assembled. He looked over above the empty street; he leaned out into the dank night air. Imperatively, he bleated: "Mr. Ortman? Oh, Mister Orrrrrrtt—man? Sir???" But there was no response; the skulking silence in the Venice night was resolute. Reluctantly, he withdrew his unkempt locks from the sill, and from what I could gather, there was one last volley of topics offered around the table. Desperate clarion calls to the Poet's hotline? Could they dial the number of his psychic cell phone? It sounded like they didn't even know the area code:

"The bombs bursting!"

"Dresden!"

"Hanoi!"

"BAG—DAD."

As the endgame was invoked, I marched across the street, just a number of steps to my dwelling. I was almost at the front door.

"GETTYSBURG!!"

"TRE-BLINKA!"

"NAGA-FUCKING-SAKI, man!!!"

"GIT-MO!!!!"

"GRANADA..."

But eventually all the screaming faded into undiscernible grunts and moans. And it was all unrated.

AOK PEST CONTROL
MAY 2008

Too many durn roof rats and colonies of meeces traipsing up and down the outside walls. More than annoying, fleeting feet and claws, plague or deer mouse virus notwithstanding. Something's gotta give, so y'open up the yellow pages and first on the list is AAA Bug Exterminators. Then comes Aaron's Bug and Pests. Then AOK Pest Control. Third to the end was Ramon's Rat Ridders, then Vic's Varmint Removal, and last but not least was Zed the Terminator. Hard choice, but I threw my towel in with AOK. And that was just, like, a-okay with me.

The dude answering the call from his mobile phone sounded like a crusty ol' geezer and claimed "thar just ain't been a job I'd a had where Mr. Rat wan't sent packin'."

His name was Jensen. Orville Jensen. And right off the bat Mr. Orville explained that "AOK" really means "Alive or Killed," 'cause he's not one of those "let's wipe 'em all out" type o' guys. He's apparently "a-filliated" with a kinder/gentler creed of pest riddance folks—only as a last resort do you "'nihilate alla' the goddamn vermin once and for all." He threw me his card. It said:

Alive **Or K**illed Pest Control

That's **A.O.K.** for **You** and **Me**

Head Exterminator: Orville Jensen

He wrenched back the parking brake and jumped outta the cab of his beat-to-crap truck. We trade shakes, and I 'splain the gravity of the situation. Well, the first order of business here is to assess if, in fact, there *is* a situation. One that needs to be addressed right away. But after being briefed of the grim reality, Orville rubs his scraggly jowls. "Rats gotta go, they do," he proclaims. "We can set traps or flush 'em out, gotta get to the nests," he announces even more resolutely. "That's whar the action is, whar it all takes place, in them nests." He looks at me, as if it's now my move, and asks, "Alive or killed?" He offers that he'd "push for killed" in this case because it "looks like y'all gotta one big fat-assed rat hotel out here. I'd strongly recommend you send their souls to hell." This advice was courtesy of kinder and gentler pest assassins. And, before you can say D-Con, Ol Orville's already hatched several options for "total a-nihilation."

But first we took a break. He broke out his lunch from an ol' crumpled Albertson's bag as we went over the "d-tails." What does a rat e-rat-icator eat? Greasy sardines on old, stale white bread, coupla carrots, and a box o' raisins. Potato chips. I.e. rat food! Some choco chips cooks for d-sert. We got sorta friendly, and he started rapping off tales (tails?) of the trade. Some of these were just doozers.

"Ah guess it was mah first rat trappin' gig," he allowed. "Oh, man, it was hell on this dear earth. Rats got inside the res'dence in the couches, all over the place. Just gross, man. We flushed 'em out with bait and some traps, but couldn't get rid of all the nests. Goddamn pack rats. Ah tell ya, wa'n't a pretty sight."

"So what was the next step?"

"We 'vacuated the folks in the house, kicked 'em out for a few days so's we could spray a fiiiine mist throughout the joint. That paralyzes the suckers. They cain't move or crawl away, just makes 'em shit all over themselves before they spaz out and die. So the vermin, they literally belly up, but then ya gotta clean up the rat crap with

Gregg Turner

alla the stiffrat corpses—and they're like everywhere. That's the part I really don't like, man."

"Wow."

"Yeah, well, that ain't nothin'. We do anything it takes, here at AOK, to send Mr. Rat packin'. Thar was the time, this fellow, his toolshed was *n*-fested. We coulda doused the whole deal in poison, but he didn't wanna go for that. Check *this* out, we jest tossed a few bull snakes that we'd had for a while, actually they were my nephew's pet snakes, *ha, ha, ha*, tossed 'em in the shack there, and when we came back in a coupla weeks, we had some fat snakes, y'know what I'm sayin'?"

He munched the last swallow from the sandwich. Swigged a mouthful of Pabst ("Don't mind if I slurp a brew or two, do ya?"). Then he cased the joint. Pointed out all of the hidey spots where "Mr. Rat could be doin' his thang... But don't you worry none, we'll get him and all of his neighborhood pals, you hear me?"

Said he once *ate* Mr. Rat. Just on a dare, but he figured it was time, after "slaughtering thousands," that he found out what Mr. Rat tasted like. Hard to argue with logic that solid. And he said that one time, after zeroing in on the nest, "Ah jest jammed my foot down on that mound of dirt and sawdust and he takes off like a goddanm bolt o'lightnin', *ha, ha*. But ah had a shard of a splintered window frame in my hand and ah gave chase, man. Ah finally lunged at the sucker and impaled his belly with the wood sliver. Boy, that was a rush! Then ah took the dead carcass and wrapped up Mr. Rat in a shirt that ah had in the back of my truck. When ah got home, didn't know whether to nuke the sucker or boil its ass, or barbeecue it. *Ah* mean, ah dinnin't wanna get the byoo-bonic plague or nothin', thought ah better cook it real good, y'know what I'm sayin'? Ah decided to nuke it 'cause that was quick an ah thought that, y'know, those microwaves can kill jest about anything, so ah nuked him to a crisp, ah did."

"Did you eat the whole thing?"

"From tail to toe. Ah doused the motherfucker with a whole bunch o' barbecue sauce 'cause I wa'n't sure what ah was getting into taste-wise, if you know what ah mean.

An if truth be told, ah really wouldn't tell anyone to do this kinda thing. The meat was grizzled like burnt rubber and ah shoulda prob'ly got ridda the gizzards, but ah figgered what the frick, y'know? Ah shoved the whole fucker in my mouth, ah did, and in one swaller downed the leathery mess into my gullet. The sauce wa'n't at all bad, but after 'bout five or so minutes ah heaved it up, ah jest blew out mah guts and regurgitated the beast into the goddamn terlet. Whooo-ey. Lesson learned, y'hear me? The aftertaste was something sicker than sick. Like licking up stale toenail clippings or something really foul, man. Ah kin still to this day feel that rubbery rodent's flesh between mah teeth. Don't go chowin' down on them vermin, *ha, ha, ha!*"

Well, it turned out Mr. Orville Jensen's a talented guy, used to be—are you ready for this?— an *Elvis impersonator* in Reno, Nevada. Didn't believe him when he first confessed, but as he was spraying a stream of pesticide along the corner of the roof, he broke into "Love Me Tender," and let me tell ya, it was good, real darn good take. Nowadays he uses the rat sprayer as a prop, and the whole act could be an Andy Kaufman routine of hick-nebbish rat eater to a pest-spraying improv Elvis. Purty impressive, there. He makes no apologies for the pest annihilation digression to El, says he doesn't really miss the "bright lights in Reno" all that much. But the Elvis routine helps his "focus."

Still, rats are rats, and that's all I really cared about, e-raticatin' the varmints.

"Heartbreak Hotel" for them. And that's when I got to meet the son. Son of AOK, Orville's seed. Name was Johnny. Johnny Jensen. And he has one pearl of a story to tell too.

"Yup, wal me and Pa, we ain't been together since I was a little kid." He recounts this sitting on the hood of his pa's truck, waiting for the initial spraying to resume. "I was a lost soul, I was. I just turned thirty, but when I was a teenager, I got into some heavy stuff. Not drugs or drinkin' or nothin', though I sorta got strung out sniffin' spray bottles of oven cleaner and other stuff like that. I was just an angry kid, getting into a lotta trouble with the law and all that. By the time I dropped outta high school, I worked on a hog farm and pitched slop. You just never smelled shit that foul. I still can't get the sound of those screamin' swine outta my ears. More than one time I fell into the hog shit pool, y'know, the shit lagoons where it all collects. It was that last time that I damn fell right down into the sewage, my face nose down in the pig X-crement, that I decided I'd had enough. Enough of that crap, *ha*. Wal, I turned my life around right then and there. I'm not sayin' I found Jesus in the hogshit cesspools, but I found *somethin'* there. Maybe it was Jesus. Hard t'say, I guess."

Johnny squinted to focus, then continued. "So then ah had this gig, workin' as a C-curity guard at a shoppin' mall in Phoenix. The whole ten yards, I was even packin' heat, they let you do that in Arizona. But one day, went into the can, there I was standing up at the yurnal and all, and I hear this explosion: BANG!! And for the life of me, I couldn't figger out what happened. I thought someone had been shot, 'cause it sounded a lot like a gun, and then I realized I was right. It was *me*. My fuckin' piece discharged into my groin as I was takin' a long-assed leak. Ah mean, the whole yurnal was dripping red, and someone called 911 and the next thing ah knew, I was in an ambulance riding real fast to the hospital.

"By the time the dust settled, I was laid up for five months, couldn't really move and all, and I hadda quit my job as C-curity guard at the mall. Sucks 'cause that was maybe the best job I ever had. Everyone was really friendly with me and all, and when I was in the hospital, my supervisor even sent me this funny get well card. It said, 'Now don't go shootin' your weenie off next time, *ha, ha, ha, ha.*' That was Mr. Pervis, he's a real funny guy. Actually the bullet didn't go anywhere near *there*, wal, close enough I suppose, but Mr. Pervis, he had a weird sense of humor. An' I knew I musta been doin' a real heads-up job 'cause he never jokes around with *anyone!*"

Johnny Orvilleseed took a deep breath and nodded matter-of-factly. "Y'see, my pa and me, we've been estranged, just like strangers, for our whole lives. Ma's down in Phoenix, but he don't pay respects to her hardly never. So we been separated our whole lives. Then when my gun discharged, we sorta got back in touch and now it's been like we never been apart! He's teachin' me the trade, how to X-terminate vermin and all sorts o' bitin' ants and wasps and what have ya. Gotta give my pa credit for opening up his heart to me; I was in a bad way. And I think I like this a whole helluva lot more than hogs or shopping malls. Just tryin' now to really be a darn good pest ridder."

At that point, Pa Jensen yapped out that he'd found one, found a nest, and lookit how "Mr. Rat is jest hidin' under the box in his spot hopin' no one's onto his hidey place."

Orville started frantically scooping out handfuls of sawdust and shavings and mud to get to Mr. Rat. But then he turned to the son, and he said this is where he "should take over. Good experience for ya." So with hands cupped, son Johno started shoveling out copious quantities of dirt under the box, but all of a sudden he started *shrieking*, shaking off a veritable army of ants that were crawling through the muck, now marching up his arms and shirt.

"FUCK, FUCK, SHIT, Daddy, Daddy, HELP! HELP ME!" But Daddy sensed that this was more appropriately time for a lesson, breaking the young'un into the business in the right way and all. So he screamed back, while Johnny is shaking, now truly convulsive, to purge all the ants and a whole gang o'black spiders hanging from strands of his hair.

"HEY THAR," screamed Pa Orville, "What did ah say about acting like a *woman*? Y'act like a girly-girl in front of the customers, they're gonna start calling you Miss Johnny, y'know what ahm sayin' thar?"

But Orville's progeny would have none of it, and he continued to screech, rolling on the ground, flailing hands to brush off the nasty insects. Then the dad got more than a shot pissed and started barking back, "You a *lady*, you lousy, no-good *woman*! Remember, we had a talk about this, about you actin' like a missy. If you gonna freak out like a dang girly, then go back to the goddamn truck and put on a dress or somethin'."

It was just at this moment of bliss and acrimony that the elusive Mr. Rat leapt out from under the mound of bugs and dirt and dashed down the driveway. Orville gave chase. He had his wooden shard raised above his head, bearing down on the rodent, but this time it was just too fast; Orville, he didn't stand a chance. But he sprinted all the way down the hill, and on the return trip up, he was heavy, heavy outta breath, face beet red, salivating something fierce. Miss Johnny, now seemingly cleansed of the bugs that had sought refuge on his hide and head, ran over to comfort the father who was then holding his chest and couldn't quite find his rhythm.

"Y'okay, there, Pa? Can I git you some water or somethin'?"

Elvis could hardly speak, but he barked back at the son, "Get me my cigareets from the truck."

The son hesitated and asked, "Are you shore, Pa, that's what you want? 'Cause you're pretty outta breath and..."

"God, almighty God—fuck it, gimme my cigareets from the truck, you idiot." Johnny ran to the truck and grabbed the pack of smokes lying on top of the dash, then handed them over to his pa. The dad roasted one up as he still tried to catch his breath at the same time, a neat trick. "Fuckin' rat. Ah almost had 'im. Wal, that won't happen again. If my daughter here warn't so busy prancing around like a sissified hairdresser I coulda got the sucker. But there'll be others, you wait 'n' see. Yeah, *lots* o' fuckin' rats at this job. There'll be others."

Then he barked out at the son, "Why don'tcha' make up an invoice for this job and I'll figure out an estimate, 'kay? Make yourself useful, boy." The son then followed my wife Wendy inside the house, produced an invoice pad, and started to write.

"Now, what you say is your address?"

She looks at him and fires back the numbers: "Fifty Ridge Road Lane, 87405."

He's scribbling away, then looks up and asks, "Ma'am, what city is that?"

"The one we're in right now, whaddaya think this is, Minneapolis?"

"Okay, just wasn't sure, just checkin'. And what number is the address?"

"That's fifty."

"Fifteen?"

"No, fifty."

He's scrawling something down, then starts to struggle with his pen out of ink. "Y'all got somethin' else ah kin write with? This here's sorta died, I think."

"There're some pens on the table in the laundry room, by the paintings on the wall."

"Okay, thanks, uhm... Hey, are those paintin's yours? Are you a painter?"

"Well, depends whom you ask, I suppose; you're welcome to look. They've been hangin' in that room for a while; they're pretty dirty."

The kid's face turns bright red: "Uhm, wal, I really already done seen some dirty pictures in my time, Pa even has a *Penthouse* in the truck, *ha, ha...*"

Gregg Turner

My wife looks at this dunce more than incredulous. He suddenly seems a bit embarrassed to check out the "dirty paintings" until it's explained to him that dirty just means...dirty. Old canvasses gathering tons of dust and film. Dirty paintings. But unnerved, Johnny passes on his art critique muse and defers his attention instead to nailing down the details for the invoice.

Whatever he's scrawling, it's awfully slow, and as this is dragging on, Wendy asks him about the "alive" part of the "alive or killed" strategy. "Do you use Have a Heart traps, the ones that catch and release?"

"Ma'am, I ain't sure what they're called, they're really just these empty-can type o' traps where you can catch 'em and then relocate 'em down the road. Problem is that the varmints almost always come back and... Wal," he looks around to see if the Pa is outta earshot, then whispers, "Don't tell on me, that I'm telling y'all this, but the 'alive' part's just for the customers to keep 'em happy, y'know, make 'em all feel good about themselves and all." Then he cups his mouth and whispers, "Pa kills 'em all anyway.He just empties the can into a bucket of water and watches 'em drown. Says he loves watching them things struggle and then they start fallin' below the surface when they cain't swim no more and then he counts the bubbles before they all drown. So, really, ah guess we're not all that much "Alive or Killed" Pest Control, more like "Always Killed" Pest Control, ah think."

> *"You're nothin but a hound dog, barkin; all the time.*
> *You're nothin but a hound dog, barkin' all the time.*
> *You're jest a lousy mutt, and y'ain't no friend o' mine..."*

We could hear the dad now woofing out the wrong song lyrics on the other side of the house. Actually, he now was on the roof, sprayin' and singin', really in his element. The kid started nodding too, and proudly proclaimed that when "Pa gets goin' with Elvis, why, that's bad news for Mr. Rat and Mr. Mouse. That's how he gets them all, all those rodents, y'know. They prob'ly think it really is Elvis, an' when they come out from their hidespots to see what the heck's goin' on, they don't know what's hit 'em!"

But then it's the ol' man's turn to start a'shriekin' and raising a ruckus on the roof. Apparently, a rabid rodent just gnashed him on the ankle and he was screaming foul things at the sun and the sky, and we all rushed up to see what happened, and his ankle was bleeding pretty darn profusely, and Johnny was going nuts trying to calm the pa down. We helped him off the top, down the ladder, and onto the ground, and Daddy-o is now trying to paramedic himself. In between convulsive howls, he cut through the wound ("just like a frickin' snakebite") and then—*oh, no,* this is unbelievable—he started spritzing his spray-poison on the wound itself. Claimed that ought to kill "everything and anything that's gonna get into mah blood."

The old man was rapidly unraveling, screamin' over to Johnny to get his phonebook from the truck and get the number of Vic (from Vic's Varmint Removal) 'cause "he'll know what t'do." As the ankle started to swell hideously, irradiating an almost glossy purple in the hard afternoon sunlight, Johnny scrambled to call colleague Vic. But Vic's sick, can't answer the phone, so they try their other cohort Zed (the Terminator). Zed says he's gonna rush right by, 'cause "this ain't no matter to take lightly," that we should call 911, but Orville'll have none o' that. "Zed'll know, he'll know what t'do," muttered the old man. Then he screamed at the kid for not finishing the invoice.

In a time-frozen flash, Zed came sauntering up the driveway. This guy's set of wheels is E-normous. Like a hopped-up Ram mongo-truck with all of these tanks and sprayers hanging out the back. Zed bounded out of his truck. He's a mousey (no pun) little guy (go figure) with just a chin scruff o' hair and thick Clark Kent black glasses, and he was wearing some sort of iron-like vest over his dirt-filthy wife-beater tee. He was chewing on a toothpick, and when he scrambled up to Orville, he spat it out in the air.

"Now what the fuck you go do to yourself this time, man?" He peered down at the wound. "Gee, that looks just horrible. We gotta get you to a doctor, man."

"Don't need no doc, Zed. Just some of that turpentine stuff you carry around with you." Apparently Zed had a jar of this inside the cab. No one else was entirely clear what the "turpentine stuff" is, but it reeked like a fart from a pregnant mule. Whew! Johnny was twitching and starting to come apart.

"Pa, is that like what you were telling me about the other day, what you called 'Zed's DEATH SAUCE'?" But Orville, he had commenced to just groaning and holding his leg just below the knee. Quickly, Zed inspected the wound and announced that we all gotta act quick-like. He opened the jar of juice (actually just a cup o' piss that Zed relieved himself of a week ago while he was driving), and the waft of fumes, once the cap's removed, had everyone taking cover. Holy moldy corn dog on a shit-stick! Then Mr. Zed poured half of the contents over the wound and Orville, he started freaking out and trying to get up and take off, but he just fell down again, hollerin' now decibels louder than before.

I had to scatter, couldn't take it no more. This was all getting too profusely twisted and dark, and as I ditched, I could discern the waning, monosyllabic rants and raves. Decided to call 911 on my own. Didn't want to risk liability should old Orville lose a limb to Zed's death sauce. The parameds were there in no time. Last I recall, they had ol' Orville's ankle wrapped up thick and tight while he was flirting with a shard's worth of residual consciousness. Finally, when the ambulance tailed off, was it "Blue Suede Shoes" I heard under the sirens in the distance? It all unraveled so quickly. Johnny was ridin' shotgun with the dad in the 911-mobile, and that just left Zed holding a half-empty jar of week-old piss.

He looked at me after a few minutes and mused, "Wal, they ain't gonna be comin' back fer a while. Those idiots'll probably be on ice for a few weeks now. Uh, y'want an estimate for what's left of the job? Ah kill 'em real fast and real good. Don't call me Zed the Terminator for nuthin.'"

But I had to ask: "Why not call yourself, say, 'Alex the Terminator,' or 'AAAA Terminators,' y'know, get in with those A's at the head of the listings in the book?" He scratched behind his ear and thought about this for a second, then bounced back with "why shouldn't the bottom of the listings not make you stand out just as much as the top? My real name's Ernest, and that'd put me smack in the middle, man. Besides, Ernest the Terminator sounds dickless."

Gregg Turner

HAIZMAN'S BRAIN IS CALLING!
AUGUST 2013

The shadows are drawing down on the Santa Cruz boardwalk in the late afternoon on a hot August day. The world's most incredible, bestest one-hundred-year-old wooden roller coaster, the Big Dipper (minimally maintained, so hold on tight as the track sways and creaks!), is making a lot of noise behind me. Pretty crowded today, lots of kids and haggard oldsters. Caramel apples and cheese pretzels and skanky-lookin' hawt dogs. A few unleashed pooches, skateboards, rental bikes. Spectacular ocean panorama. Fun in the California sun for almost everyone.

These three punky-lookin' gals—maybe in their early girly twenties, two have Black Sabbath tees on and one is wearing, honest to fuck, an Angry Samoans tank top—bop down the boardwalk. Tank top girl wears the photo of the chick with the axe in her head (cover pic from our first record, *Inside My Brain*—which was lifted from a still of the movie *The Black Cat*). Boy, did we get into a lot of trouble for that one. Marches in Hollywood of lady-folk protesting violence against women, holding this album cover up in the air as evidence of such a thing (my ex-wife [equals woman], she designed the cover).

So I couldn't help myself: I walk up to the one festooned in the Sam's tee. "Where'd you get this?"

She looks at me indignantly, scowls, "What's it to you?"

"That's my band! I'm a cofounding member!"

"Yeah, right," she sneers.

"No, really, I, uh, cowrote some of the songs on that record and the next one, the hardcore record, *Back from Samoa*!"

"You're so full o'shit, man." All of a sudden it seemed terribly important to make the case. She wasn't even plasma in her mommy's womb when we did our thing way back when in the eighties. But she pauses, and now even more indignant, asks me, "What was the second song on side two of *Inside My Brain*?"

I couldn't exactly remember: "Uhhmm...uhh..." She scowls. "Yeah, right."

"No, *really*, try again!"

"What song on side two is 'Haizman's Brain Is Calling'?"

"Hey, Keith Morris from the Circle Jerks likes that one!"

"Yeah, right on, like I'd believe that? So where is it on side two, man, if you know so much?"

"Well, uhhh...I think it's the, uhm, one, two, three...the fourth one on side two." Been more than a while since I picked up the effin' record.

"Just what I thought, man...gimme a freakin' break, you're a poseur wannabe. It's the *second song*, right after "Steak Knife." She looked at her Black Sabb friends. Let's split. This guy's a sorry loser. Nice try, dude."

"Wait a minute, check this out. Did you know that the King of Western Samoa was going to fly us out, to his island or whatever it is, in his personal jet, to headline a Samoan festival? It was all set. Uhm, then apparently he listened to the records. And he wouldn't talk to us no more. Maybe 'They Saved Hitler's Cock' went too far ["If Hitler's Cock could choose it's mate, it would ask for Sharon Tate!"—best lyric I ever writ]."

"Gimme a fuggin' break," she smirked.

"Or the time we were loading in to play a gig in an industrial warzone in Carson, California—in the beginning, when our following was limited to about six friends. And these honest-to-gawd, real-life angry Samoans met us in the parking lot, way PO'd, growling, asking us what our issues with Samoans were. Our bass player, Todd 'The Hippie Stabber' Homer, had the wherewithal to run to the nearest liquor store and grab a case of Mickey's Big Mouth, wretched stuff, and offer it to these mammoth-sized dudes as a peace gesture! We quickly became Samoan soul mates, and they carried our gear into the club. Told us that if we ever needed some Samoan muscle to knock anyone off, they'd be happy to oblige!"

She looked back: "In your dreams, man. Lame story." They trotted off.

The sun vanished below the sea's horizon. There was a long line to ride the Big Dipper. I felt like scarfing some serious popcorn, but the line for that was pretty long too. So I made tracks to my car in the parking lot.

TWENTY FIG NEWTONS
APRIL 1993

Mathematics legend Spencer "Spence" Atkinson was known universally for his publications and research in an area of applied analysis. His hulking stature—burly with unkempt flowing beard, generous girth, and dominating disposition—added to the larger-than-life spectacle that propelled his orbit in the math circles he traversed. He professed the subject at an elite private college, one of a consortium of elite private colleges up in New England. Famously, you might spot him scarfing down thick sausage hoagies on one of the busy streets near the schools, his white facial hair suddenly stained brown with greasy sausage sauce draining symmetric down his jowls.

Mathematicians often come in two flavors. Atkinson was of the Rasputin inclination—his wild chalkboard gesticulations and accelerated, sometimes manic and thunderous expository lectures to his class provided great theater. His colleague, Janos Heidelberg, was another charter member of this Rasputin tribe—he would lecture with both hands at the same time. The right hand furiously scripted the equations on the board, with such force that chalk fragments would splinter, while the left hand sculpted intricate pictures and graphs associated with the equations the right hand was transcribing. Simultaneously! More remarkable were the times when the left hand got sections ahead of the material the other hand was presenting. Ha! The other flavor, the mathematical disposition that leans to the more anal-retentive side of the spectrum, can be witnessed in the bundled-up affectations of tidiness and OCD-like behavior of Harold Brower, for example. He doesn't care for the chalk dust collecting all over his fleshy paws when he lectures at the board. So he has metal chalk holders fastened to each piece—his bow tie is precisely mounted to his shirt's white collar. If you venture into his office, the papers on his desk are selectively arranged in organized stacks, right next to the little boxed containers of pencils and paper clips. And erasers.

But Spence's gregarious gyrations lecturing to his class conjured more the tornado of a whirling dervish of angst and freaky kinetic energy! Whilst scrawling intricate proofs on the board, students' hands go up, questions are asked. Spence spins around to address the confusion. As he exhales explanation, one arm with chalk is gesticulating emphatically the mathematical details in the air. Though all in the class are flummoxed trying to follow this, Spencer, satisfied he has adequately addressed the point, whirls back to the board to continue. This ritual repeats several times but then, caught up in the commotion and turmoil, Professor Atkinson becomes confused. Although he is still facing the class, his back to the blackboard, he resumes lecturing in the air. The strains of incredulity that abound from clueless students who can't quite catch the drift are palpable—Spence is just transfixed disseminating theory to a wormhole in space and time.

He has blood sugar issues. Around five in the afternoon he has trouble keeping his orbs open. If you come to his office around that time, you'll catch him on the nod, head drooping over freshly scrawled notes, graded papers, and partially masticated cheese sandwiches. But at four in the afternoon every Wednesday the consortium of colleges hosts the weekly math colloquium. Three thirty to four is the time for cookies and coffee. Then four to five thirty a visiting guest speaker presents a new theorem or two in front of faculty and graduate students. Spence munches copious quantities of carbs and black coffee, then traipses off to the lecture hall and plants himself down in the third row. But the sugar high spikes quickly and in a heartbeat crashes precipitously as the speaker starts etching equations on the board.

Now there are many, *many* specialties of research in mathematics. And at this level of specialization and expertise, the technical details and symbolism from one area can differ markedly from that of other areas. For example, discourse in analytic number theory may not register to the mathematical synapses of the expert in thirteen-dimensional topology. Nevertheless, despite the implicit understanding of those attending the presentation that they may not be able to follow the technicality, it's all good. Everyone basks in the glory of the intellectual math porn feverishly scrawled out in manic waves.

Professor Atkinson was an established presence and revered math icon for decades; he was popular and well acquainted with colleagues all over the world. So when he passed out in sublime nodness, three minutes into the guest speaker's lecture, it wasn't particularly invasive, so no bones to pick. But then rapidly came the sounds of the exorcist in a semi sleep-frozen state, these train-wrecked grunts and moans and incantation-like sputterings. This could go on for a few minutes, and ultimately dissipate. Or the sound tsunami might escalate and ejaculate into ungodly tirades of Gregorian chanting! Because of his renown, incredibly, each of the weekly presenters would pretend they didn't hear or really notice anything. They just ignored the sonic holocaust like nothing was happening and would continue with the lecture. All this as Spence continued to succumb to some crazy REM downtime and sputter.

Professor Emeritus Jeremy Rothschild was eighty-one years old. In retirement he solved an outstanding problem of two hundred years. Not only was the solution believed to be intractable (unproven theorems in mathematics are shelved as mere "conjectures"), his age disqualified the popular notion that solving intransigent open problems is a young person's game. Snidely, one hears amongst mathematicians that after age thirty one is relegated to proving corollaries (no longer theorems!). So the fact that this veteran oldster was able to accomplish such a feat heartened the cockles of the math community of academes. That and the fact that this particular result was considered quite significant allowed for a good deal of attention. It was to be published in a prestigious peer-reviewed journal in a few months. Many colleges and universities reached out to Professor Rothschild to bless their school with a preliminary outline of the solution and its proof (which apparently was quite long). But at Smithson College, where Atkinson resided, another faculty associate knew the old guy personally. That connection trumped others, and so the exposition of the Rothschild Condition for stabilization of chaotic systems of delay differential equations was slated to be delivered at the college's colloquium not far in the future.

This was going to be a big deal. Faculty and graduate students from across the area from the most esteemed academic institutions were planning on being there. The presentation was to be moved to a lecture auditorium at one of the larger schools in the five-college consortium (of which Smithson was a part). The date was finally set to great fanfare, with press widely circulating announcement of the event.

The only fly in the proverbial ointment was, well, Spence's somnambulistic eruptions. How to control this? It just wouldn't be seemly to have an auditory firehose of freshly flavored guttural incantations from the third row of the auditorium disrupting the affair. So this was a concern.

"Maybe if we feed him copious quantities of cookies and black coffee that'll keep him going," one colleague offered.

"We could spike the punch with Adderall," another one half-jokingly mused.

"We need a system, a strategy here," still another faculty member offered. After some discussion, they decided that the "strategy" would involve planting a colleague in the seat next to Spence—if he became disruptive in the throes of catatonia, this adjacent fellow or fellow-ette would jab him in the arm or stomp on his foot. Gently. He was, after all, Dr. Spencer Atkinson.

So that was the plan, as feeble as it might sound.

Twenty Fig Newtons and three cups of black coffee had Spence buzzing as he walked down the steps of the engineering auditorium to his (usual) third row seat. His butt collapsed in the cushioned chair, and speaking of buzzing, the air in the room was swollen with amped expectations and heavy anticipation of the presentation of this Rothschild Condition. Seats were filling up.

The problem with twenty Fig Newtons and three cups of coffee is that the sugar spike is tenuous and the resultant crash is a waterfall. So after becoming comfortable in his seat, uh oh, his eyes grew heavy. Madeleine Bouchard, math faculty at nearby Pennington College and longtime friend and colleague, hunkered down in the cushion next to Spence. She knew what to do, if it came to that.

Professor Rothschild slowly marched down the steps of the auditorium to the front of the room, up to the massive paneled blackboards. There he was, a charter member of the anti-Rasputin sect of math-professing folks. Bow tie, slacks, white dress shirt under tweed coat. A thinning layer of well-groomed white hair crowning nose and face. And, of course, metal holders fastened to fifteen pieces of chalk laid out in the trays attached to the boards. There were three sliding panels of boards, on small wheels, so that a filled board could be rolled up to the top to make room for the next empty board. The lights radiating down on the paneled boards suddenly intensified, room lights dimmed. And Spencer's eyes grew heavy and he passed out sublimely. His head bowed. He was gone.

Rothschild started at the top of the lower paneled board on the left (there were three columns of boards). Before transcribing anything, he waved to the rapt group of mathematicians packed tight in the room. In turn, everyone stood up and applauded. Spence was snoozing, now glued to his seat, head heavy to the floor. Dr. Rothschild selected a piece of metal-protected chalk to commence.

He began sketching the equations; these were elucidated carefully and slowly. But the handwriting was so incredibly microscopic (and messy—hardly legible) that anyone beyond the first row squinted tightly to impossibly discern the details. Soon the first board was filled and ensconced with figures and abstractness that few could follow.

Boards were subsequently wheeled up and down. Nothing erased, just a continuity of symbolism and more and more detail. Third board up, fourth board down—fifth board. This happened in real time quickly. Some folks were jotting notes, though it strained credulity that anyone could succinctly eyeball the equations from any distance in the room to even begin the note-jotting process. The writing was just so tiny.

And then it started. The sleeping beast erupted and growled in fury. "Aaaughh. EEGahhh, ECHHH OGKGJWSODMG!!!" Bouchard stomped on Spencer's foot and that seemed to temporarily suspend the onslaught. It decayed into rapturous snoring and then he passed out again and the presentation resumed. The speaker was taken aback for a second and stared contemptuously at the slumbering Spence. Ironically, he and Atkinson had yet to cross paths in real life conferences or even socially. So, unlike other guest speakers who were familiar with this strange show and ignored its transmission, Rothschild was caught off guard—he had not a clue who this momentarily obtrusive presence in the third row could be. But politely he continued—and then a few minutes later it happened again.

This time the crazy sounds beckoned the hounds of hell! Bestial grunts from the dark side and tortured ravings exploded with a massive seismic footprint and emanated louder and more obstructive than even before. More stomps on his slumbering feet, but that only provoked a bigger shitshow of foul decibels. "*GUHHH, AWERGA MEEEGAHH*!!" Then the catatonic cacophony of symphonic night-like terrors just detonated: "BASTARDS, YOU'RE ALL BASTARDS, GODDAMIT." He was vomiting gibberish loudly, eyes closed, still very fast asleep.

Blackboard seven was just filled. And Atkinson's from-the-dead sonic infusion into the air could no longer be ignored. The speaker whirled around.

"Perhaps the rude fellow making disgusting sounds in the third row has noticed some error in the details."

The reverent crowd gasped. BIG STOMP on the foot this time and that seemed to stir life into the sleeping giant. "Spencer, STOP IT. Shut up." She jostled his shoulder.

He looked up, neurotransmitters suddenly kick-started. Eye contact was cemented with the speaker. With a few loud snorts, Spence looked around, more than disoriented. The old man was severely pissed off now, and retorted loudly, "I wasn't aware that these lectures admitted members of the custodial staff."

Oh, shit. The only thing larger than the girth of the sleeper was his unrelenting ego! NO ONE dares to call him the janitor! This required response. He bolted upright in his seat: "Whaa... Okay. Your proof is wrong, it's all fucked up!"

Cascading waves of horror crashed upon the brows of faculty in the auditorium. "Spencer, you're making an ass out of yourself. Shut up," Bouchard, next to him, snarled. This material wasn't close to his area of expertise, so even conscious it would be unclear he'd be able to follow the nuances. His eyes had been tightly sealed the entire time. And the speaker's insect-like scrawl, the ant-like writing, was hardly fathomable anyway! But now Spence (abruptly) assumed an erect posture, eyes now very wide open.

Rothschild shot back, "Perhaps the janitor would like to identify any errors on the board?"

Atkinson glared at the layout of the equations; clearly this was his very first focus of the sprawled-out equations spanning six boards. He was in deep now, needed to save face, so he retorted loudly, "Well, the second to last line you just scribbled out contradicts, let's see, the one, two, three…the fifth line on the second board up there. They're incongruous. So it's all messed up. It's just wrong!"

"Spencer, STOP THIS," Bouchard pleaded next to him, "you sound like a fool." The entire room was silent—this was terribly painful for all to watch. Nevertheless, the old-timer looked back at the board and for-real (remarkably!) spotted an error—which he quickly corrected. Everyone in the room squinted to catch the imperfection. Even with binoculars you could hardly read the writing, so, so small. He erased two or three symbols and stared down the "janitor."

He smirked, "I apologize for the error—but that's all it is…"

Spence grimaced, then bellowed, "NO GO: With that correction, it now contradicts the—let's see, the seven, eight, nine…tenth line down the first, second—THIRD board. And that means the whole result is totally fucked up."

The elderly academician whirled back to the third board and fixed the equation that Spence has singled out. "*Okay,*" he proclaimed, "*that takes care of that!*" Satisfied he had remedied the "incongruity," he intended to resume the lecture. But then someone in the second row pointed out that this change now invalidates the conclusion on the last line of board five.

Finally, someone way in the back yelped out, "<u>THIS IS NOT FIXABLE</u>!" And she explained why and how any change that is now made would invalidate everything else. "The logic is injured!" There was a collective gasp in the air, and if a quarter dropped on the plush carpet out in the ornate Hall of Newton past the back row, you would have heard it rattle!

"Well," the speaker intoned just as quietly, "I don't recall this being a problem before, and certainly referees from the *Journal of Applied Mathematics* found no issue—I...I...I..." His voice trailed off. "Well, I need to think about this for a bit..." He bowed his head slightly and asked to be a given a "moment to reflect." Then he ambled up the steps of the auditorium and hobbled in a humbled gait out into the hall, which was on the third floor and had a ledge with a sheer drop to a cement patio below. Two graduate students were quickly dispatched to make sure no tragic event might transpire.

Still hushed silence, a few nervous chatters—and then, and then, somewhere emerging from the front came the horrible, thunderous stench of familiar sound: "ASD@#$XC...ECCHHHHH... BASTARDS...GODDAMMIT, ALL BASTARDS..." His eyes were fast closed, had been for the last five or ten minutes during the clamor of desperate audience attempts to rectify the details. When the guttural claptrap of this sleep-spew trailed off, he began to snore heavily, his weary head resting on the shoulder of Madeleine Bouchard, the next seat over.

LET THE COLORS FLOW!
SEPT 1996

American culture ad nauseum. At nauseum. You want vengeance for capital crimes: replace lethal injections with forced sampling of Katy Perry or (even worse) Howie Mandel-imposed sightings of *America's Got Talent* (eyelids à la *Clockwork Orange* forced open to take in a revolving looped specter; whatever happened to John Davidson?). We have reached, ladies and gentlemen, the equilibrium point, the homeostasis of laissez-faire capitalism on the free market of culture: art evolved (in the Darwinian sense of market dynamics) as a *forced enema*. Now, when you think musical forced enema, e.g., the mind's eye generally gravitates to, say, Joan Baez. But I'm talking something substantially more insidious as a *process*.

There's an appropriate metaphor (as processes go) that may help to amplify all of this. Some time ago, 1993, I relocated to a place that (rather gratuitously) calls itself "The City Different," Santa Fe, New Mexico (been here since; although somewhere in the interim, like 1998–1999, with aspirations of jump-starting a stalled and constipated career as a collegiate math academe, I accepted a gig at Clark University [Siggy Freud's only US college-campus talk-stop when he visited stateside] which required relocation to what must be one of the most strychnine swallowed swill pits in the entire country—Worcester, Massachusetts—an incredible underbelly of urban blight. A city built upon its own societal bile—but I digress).

In 1996 (still in SF)—you won't believe this!—I managed to sneak onto the AM radio talk-show airwaves! KVSF ("The Voice") 1260 AM, only talk-radio on the dial with mostly bad syndicated pipe-ins (the late Dr. Laura, etc.) during the week, but Saturday and Sunday, it's free-for-all time. Here's how it worked. Pitch a concept to the station manager. If he grooves, then you're ON! and ON! means one hour (at the assigned time slot) each weekend. What's the catch, you ask? Okay, okay, it costs sixty-five dollars (*you* pay *them*). But that's a pretty cheap donation for an hour of LIVE (no delay) radio, potential listening audience of 100,000. Just two sponsored ads at only $32.50 each would cover the price tag. So I proposed the following concept: *Howard Stern meets the X-Files*, e.g., alien-abducted dwarfs and so forth (figured there had to be at least two of these in Santa Fe, which is nutjob-central. Roswell, New Mexico, three hours southeast of town, has the Alien Museum and the yearly saucer abduction conferences, but Santa Fe can be something else—like California's Venice Beach boardwalk on bad acid); serious abductees wishing to remove their rectally probed implant devices (Art Bell one better, eh?). Most of my other weekend colleagues (quickly they were more than embarrassed to regard me as such) on the 1260 band did stuff like "Responsible Crystal Energy—Only When It Is Called For," "God's Green Gardening," or "Homeopathic Love Rites," etc.

We called the show The *Different* City Different and we were ON! from 3:00 to 4:00 p.m. Sunday afternoons. We had real, honest-to-god *graverobbers* (proper shoveling technique and what to do when you first "hit coffin"), as well as the standard cadre of alien abducts (one was introduced to her three hybrid "bearded" alien children)—this one woman described her reward for putting up with "what must have been hours" of examination: an alien-induced orgasm in the saucer's command control center.

Swiftly we got into trouble when, the first time, we brought on these dominatrix/bondage fetishers from Albuquerque. Warned not to do it again ("This is a Hispanic, Catholic city, and you're launching leather sex deviants on *Sunday*?" the station manager was apoplectic). More dire fallout: the one (and only!) sponsor (fifty dollars, though!), Middle Eastern Cuisinarts, the Sphinx Café, they asked us to play along with the show's theme. Well, at least the boheme coowner who thought it'd be funny to advertise "whipping up an appetite for tabouleh." Actually, the on-air ad played out: "I dunno about you," I announce to my cohost Dave, "but when my dominant is chasing me around the block and I know that my rump is gonna get one helluva WHACK—some serious red-ass—I'm thinking falafel balls— at the Sphinx Café!"

"Yeah, I hear you," gloats Dave, who not-so-reluctantly chimes in with, "When my submissive's screaming for mercy, I'm counting on scarfing some serious hummus—and the only place to do that is at the Sphinx Café." Et cetera. Unfortunately, the Sphinx beatnik's born-again (ex-marine) lamb-kabob partner did not share the humor, so no more grape-leaf comps—or ad money. And possibly a big-time lawsuit for emotional distress and defaming Jesus.

We slogged on for nine months (fitting gestation for a beginning and an end)—the second time the bondage gals came on, we had a "forced feminization and live spanking" on the air. I think we could have slipped through the censor's knot (station manager, uhm, gave us margin—at least enough so that he seldom sampled what the hell was going on) even this time around. 'Cept in the last two or three minutes, the gruff, expansively large dominatrix known as the Goddess Glory, who had been wailing on a volunteer's buttocks, live on-mike, to demonstrate proper spanking etiquette ("folks out in radio land probably don't understand just how crucial it is to come down somewhere between thirty-five and forty-five degrees to the crack of the butt; more than fifty degrees is way too much trauma, less than thirty degrees is not sufficient reinforcement!"), became suddenly agitated and declared her subject to be a "bad slave." She then resolutely announced that she was prepared for this eventuality; a black medical bag was produced (where did this come from?) and our slave was threatened with a horse-sized colonic. The slave, up till this point—a good sport, one of our guys just playin' along— had been decked out in bra and panties and lipstick for his "forced feminization." Still all this talk about slavish reprisal unnerved the poor guy and, taking no chances (rectal probes s'posed to be part of the *alien* show, not the slave segment), bolted out of the studio smack into the middle of Sunday rush-hour on St. Francis Boulevard. But the Goddess was ready. There were two other slaves, the ones *she* brought with her in tow that day, and some loser in gold chains who called himself "Lord Tristan." With our forced-feminized slave absent and sprinting down the street now far from harm's way, the Goddess Glory summoned one of the slaves in her entourage this time.

"OPEN THAT MOUTH AND EAT MOMMY'S PUSSY!" Uhhh, can you say "PUSSY" live on AM radio? The red phone next to the recording booth started to erupt and illuminate. I had never even noticed it before. Apparently this is the station manager's hotline, and boy is he hot! Shrieking, screaming, seizures, blah blah blah. "That's the END," he wailed. "You're SO outta here. EAT MOMMY'S PUSSY on live radio? What the eff are you thinking?" But I really wasn't thinking too clearly at this point; I managed to beg for another chance. I guess the problem was that the gardening show, "Bless The World, Bless Your Plants," decided to throw in the towel and never come back. Oh, well. We had great ratings at that point. But no more sponsors—they were just too chickenshit.

Mad Mary Williams, this marginally gestated homunculus, was a sometimes sweet, sometimes nasty crackpot and semi-local loon

Gregg Turner

who once ran a locally looned-out restaurant known as Mad Mary's Market and Bistro. Here, patrons swung the most to alternative late-night psychedelic food vibes. Mary in past cycles of existence claimed tenure as seamstress for the Grateful Dead, as well as being a celluloid extra eager to gregariously munch on sheep spleens ("we had fake organ props for all of the extras, but she chewed on *real* ones," maintains the producer of the original *Night of the Living Dead)*. The woman was charged with more than paranormal life force—and the groovy holistic holocaust of her establishment saturated the ambiance and rafters, wafting generously throughout the place.

Stories traded hands about patrons admonished for selecting food not color compatible with the wavelength their souls dialed. And rumor had it that the process for hiring new help, kids usually from nearby schools, was to ask them to eat raw meat from dog dishes on the ground! The place was like some dark, orgiastic hippie hayride that'd run amuck, a cartoon underbelly of backwashed peace and love right back in your face, brother! She was an "empath" and could discern whether or not your kishkas were riddled with parasites. Roundworms, tapeworms, flat worms—these were the usual cult of invaders diagnosed upon Mad Mary's most momentary tableside meditations and reflection. Then for a nominal fee, a couple hundred bucks or so, she'd de-lice you and rid your organs and bowels of all intruding varmints. A medical miracle worker, no less.

But there were other issues as well. She'd been banned, at that time, from twenty-six restaurants in town. Not clear what the exact circumstances were that promulgated her to the top of the fork-and-knife eviction list—some say she'd been overly demanding and fussy with seating placement (necessary to capture just the right gastric energy), or maybe it was food returned to the kitchen consecutive times. Restaurant managers just couldn't get her drift. So with this angle, we decided to actually launch the very first show and promote with a poster that read something like:

PROPHET OR PARIAH
... MENACE OR MESSIAH
BANNED FROM 26 LOCAL EATING ESTABLISHMENTS
*WILL **YOURS** BE NEXT*?!!

For preproduction, we decided that we'd treat the woman and her boyfriend to dinner at Poulet Gourmet, then a high-end chic eatery near the downtown hotels. We taped the adventure, just in case we were privy to Banning Number Twenty-Seven, to capture the psychodrama live. But, of course, nothing to capture. Not only nada eviction from the premises, she and the boyfriend were delightfully cheerful and hospitable to waitstaff, no complaints about the food— only the tab, which amounted to just over $300, remained as the night's lone witness to a debauchery-free meal. We'd been chumped! Never imagined that we'd even get past the appetizers!

So we dig deeper. Something must be going on. Twenty-six dead-on dining evacuations had to leave a veritable trail of lobster bisque blood *somewhere*...roundworms in the crepes? Not enough chakra in the okra? Then we got a tip: Chef Gregoire from the elegant trendy Frenchy bistro, Melange, said he'd talk. Was willing to rap vitriolic on air why she'd been booted from *his* place. In his thick accent de francais, he recounts:

"Well, so they seet down at ze end of ze room. She starts een immediate-ly about ze water, how eet has not been, what you say, cleansed. Of course, I do not know what zis means, ze cleanseeng of ze water. She says sometheeng about a blesseeng—and why does my water need to be blessed, I have never heard such a zing. And zen she just goes cra-zeee. They need to changes places weeeth the crippled couple at ze table on ze ozzer side. Something about energy, how do you say, swap? My waitress, she throws up her hands and zen reefuzez to serve zem. And what am I to say? But I treat all my customers weeth respect, and so we still humor zem. But zen when ze food comes, and she starts going ze crazy about ze garneesh weeth ze entrée, then I just blow up my fuse. I have never ever had ze complaints about ze garneesh put on ze plates! She was, how do you say, a butthole!"

Interesting. Mad Mary in studio live on air is now furiously nodding up and down to this incantation of gourmet horror.

Ech. Eeet turned ugly.

Mad Mary Williams had a neighbor. She was a grave robber, so she claimed. We couldn't help it, she was the next guest the following week discussing proper corpse plunging prowess and the thrill of it all when you "hit coffin." Before you could scream Herschell Gordon Lewis, she was letting us know about all the booty she'd wielded from down under. But other than the "adrenaline high," which apparently promoted return visits to the corpse fields, she conceded it was a "stinky business." Okay.

Then there was Black Bear. He asked to have his voice altered and entered the studio in a humongous gorilla outfit. Said he had secret info from the fabled Area 51 to share. He'd been there recently, of course, and said the world needed to know just what was going on. The gorilla costume and voice tweak—to supposedly protect him from the feds who've been actively after him for the last several months—were ridiculous. It was a risk, he conceded, appearing on the radio, but one he was willing to take for the sake of making folks savvy about nefarious activities being played out in the high desert of Nevada.

Bear saunters into the studio ten minutes late, a gorilla mask on top of a densely tufted body piece of brown fur—black gorilla head and brown fur ape suit. We didn't really have any audio effects to alter his voice, so we stuffed napkins in his yap (through the mouth hole in the mask). Just what goes on in the fabled Area 51? What secrets are obfuscated from the public? What's all this about?

He looks down at the ground, then gets into it: "When I broached the security fence, this giant concrete wall with razor-wire laced over the top, I realized it would be challenging to break on through, at least to hoist myself over the top. So I kept thinking, thinking, thinking... Then it hit me—I'll just go through the front entrance like anyone else."

No high security clearance needed?

"Ah thought about that, but when I got to the front, you wouldn't believe it—no one there in the booth—empty! So I sprinted to the very first building I could eyeball. The door was ajar, and I lunged into what looked to be some sorta closet. It had these glowing jars. I knew immediately what was inside each one—alien embryos. Then there were larger specimen jars of little baby critters. Mottled faces, tiny horns. Ah made mah way through an adjacent, it seemed like a tunnel, to another, narrower room; there was a giant white refrigerator."

Was it opened, I asked, what was in there?

"Yes, I quickly opened the door. Just a stack of Mrs. Smith pies. So I slammed the door shut, ran out to a much larger room—and THAT was when I lost mah shit."

Can this be shared with our listeners?

"Yes. I will. Okay, you asked for it: There was a woman in her middle ages, slightly portly. She was stripped and fastened to a vertically standing table. The big sergeant came out. I call him that because he had on a military uniform and looked, uhm, like Murkin. Then he pulled off his pants, and..."

He continued: "The sergeant mounted her against the table, but then he had a hose, looked like a garden hose, and he squirted this slushy crap all over her face and hair. Well, she suddenly started screaming to this sergeant fellow that her husband was some bigwig

Republican politician from Kentucky [Mitch McConnell?] and that there'd be reprisals big-time. But the sergeant started squirting the green juice in her trap, and that's when I felt this, this presence—that's all I can describe it as. A presence. The hair on the back of my head spiked at attention. I felt this hot breath on the bottom of my neck. And then I passed out."

Time for a station break! "You're listening to KVSF 1260 AM LIVE radio, The Voice," I announced dutifully. "We are the *Different* City Different, and, in case you've just tuned in, we're listening to one heckofa crazy-assed report of what's inside Area 51. I, of course, can't vouch for what this gentleman, who calls himself Black Bear, has been sayin'—but it appears to be quite an abominable nightmare! Let's hear some more."

But when I looked to my side in the booth, Black Bear was nowhere-ville; apparently he *woosh*ed out the studio door during the station ID. Cohost Dave pointed to the clock; we had ten minutes left. Uhm, okay, let's take some calls.

"Hi, my name is Jamie, I live here in town, and I'm having a hard time believing ANY of this junk. This has to be a put-on, right? I mean, we're supposed to buy the fact that some deranged dude in a military uniform is jamming Mitch McConnell's wife? What idiot writes your script?"

"Now, hold on, caller," I offer, "no one's identified this woman on the gurney as the wife of ANYONE; let's make that clear. And we don't have a script writer—what this gentleman who calls himself Black Bear recounts, we do not endorse as fact or fiction."

Still, the caller can't let it go—he starts yelling over the air: "THEN WHY DID HE SQUIRT ALL THAT GREEN STUFF INTO HER FACE, WHAT THE HELL IS THAT ABOUT?"

I look at the studio clock: 3:58 p.m. Two minutes before the top of the hour, and we're outta here. Time out. "Well, thank you, caller!

Unfortunately our time is up. All of you in listener-land, please come back and join us next week, here on the *Different* City Different! Following our show is Dr. Pierre Anthony, and his program is called Healing Matters and boy, does it ever! Dave, whaddaya think?"

"Yeah, it sure does, man! My pancreas has been acting up, so I'm gonna tune in to this soon as we leave the air!"

Pierre Anthony lunges into the booth. He doesn't look particularly thrilled to be following our Area 51 reveal segment, so we make quick tracks into the parking lot.

OMG! Black Bear is being frisked against the studio wall by dudes with FBI vests! Seriously! Honest to dog! Before you can say "green squirt from a firehose," we jump in our cars and race out into the afternoon shower of sunlight beating down on St. Francis Boulevard. The feds are apparently content with their captive, and we both make mental notes not to engage with fugitives! Holy crap!

The most difficult aspect of doing such a program, the hardest thing to nuance, was relying on such notoriously *un*reliable folks. We'd broadcast live, so in the event of a no-show, we always needed to have a backup plan. This was put to the test one afternoon when Big Red failed to make it. Big Red was this tall, burly guy who sported a particularly full-sprouted red, red beard. He'd wander around town wrapped up tightly in full wedding-gown regalia, complete with a long train that was seemingly a magnet for thistles and cactus needles, holding onto a bouquet of drooping, dead flowers. They say he was a seriously riveting scribe of verse and poems, but I, uh, couldn't tell you anything about that. Word on the street was that Red was once a high-clearance Los Alamos physicist and, upon returning home from a particularly long day at the Lab, found the wife in bed with another gent and flipped his lid like a mad quark. Since that time, legend has it, he donned the wife's wedding apparel hanging in their closet and quickly assimilated icon status as a street nomad in here-comes-the-bride drag. But Big Red apparently couldn't make it to our mic that day, and there was no point stalling any further, already fifteen minutes into the broadcast.

Little choice but to open up the alternative Health Classifieds, maybe score a goofball or two on the phone. We could get lucky. Let's see...

"Warts removed in minutes?" Nah. Too pedestrian.

"Chakra Detox" (no kidding!). Uhhhh...

"Spiritual Psychic Surgery." Maybe.

"Holy Holistics," No thanks.

Oh—this one might work: "COLONIC CAFÉ LATTE REMEDY FOR ALLERGIES." Yes, let's give that a try! So, y'know, we dial, and the woman, who performs such a thing, agrees to take us through the procedure. Graphically. On the phone. For real. Jackpot!

"First," she says, "I will hold your hand and spiritually attune myself to the discordant energy in your colon. After all, you wouldn't just pick up ANY musical instrument and expect symphonic rapture without tuning first."

She has a point, I allow.

"After we are spiritually tuned, I will take you to the...wooden platform. You will lie down on your back with your garments removed and your butt cradled in the butt aperture in the table. There are now two tubes. One is for irrigation—it pumps a solution of tepid café latte and ionized spring water at room temperature. Sometimes I do it with a caramel macchiato. The other tube is for evacuation—it forcefully suctions the contents of the bowels once you have been sufficiently and adequately irrigated. There is a pail into which the evacuation tube empties. And there are mirrors placed below the platform and on the ceiling so that you are permitted, I should say encouraged, to observe all of this, while on the platform on your back. I feel it is important for my clients to know just what is being dislodged and removed. Now, I urge patients to insert both of these tubes to get the process started. However, some are reluctant and if this is the case I will assist with the initial positioning and placement. Psychologically speaking, I feel that self-insertion bolsters autonomy and self-esteem—so I really motivate my clients to...*stick 'em in!* If they are successful—or even make the attempt—I stand back and give them a BIG ROUND OF APPLAUSE! I should point out to your listeners that there can, however, be a wide range of emotion displayed. Frequently there is...weeping."

"Weeping?" Her voice began to trail and fade; the engineer, on the other side of the studio's glass partition, frantically signals to keep the woman animated. "Why weeping?"

"Weeping because—well, weeping is inevitable. When they look into the mirrors and see what comes out of their behinds—into the pail—they invariably weep. They must weep. And I weep with them. I am holding their hands and tears are streaming down my cheeks— we are weeping together because we are celebrating the joy of colonic liberation.

"JUST LAST WEEK I WEPT WITH A MAN—THIS WAS A WELL-KNOWN LOCAL POLITICIAN, BUT I WON'T MENTION ANY NAMES. A FAT ONE [*Bill Richardson?? Chris Christie??*]. HE WAS LIKE A BLOATED BEACH BALL. HE INSERTED HIS OWN TUBES. I WAS VERY PROUD OF HIM; THIS WAS A BIG FIRST STEP. WELL, BY THE TIME THE EVACUATION TUBE WAS DOING ITS DEAL, HE BEGAN TO MOAN. HE WAS A GROANING, TORMENTED SOUL. A BIG FAT COW WITH A HALF MOUTH OF CUD. THERE WAS AGONY AND LIBERATION. AND I WAS GROANING WITH HIM. WE WERE BOTH LOCKED ON THE MIRRORS. BURNING A GODDAMN PATH OF EXISTENTIAL STEAM, STARING DOWN AT THE RED AND GREEN AND PURPLE THAT WAS SPURTING OUT OF

Gregg Turner

HIS HIND AND RAPIDLY FILLING THE PAIL. YOU SEE…THESE WERE REMNANTS OF *CRAYONS* THAT HE HAD DEVOURED AS A SMALL CHILD—AND HAD IMPACTED IN HIS BOWELS FOR FIFTY-TWO YEARS!! And he was just mooooaaaanning and grooooaaanning, and I pressed the palm of my hand on his distended gut, and moaanned and groaanned with him; we were just a symphony of animal sounds; and the colors just poured out of him, such a beautiful thing to behold. SO I SAID TO HIM—

> **LET THE COLORS FLOW!**
> **LET THE BLUE LEAVE YOU!!**
> **LET THE GREEN DO ITS THING!!!**
> **OR LET THE RED COME OUT INSTEAD!!**
> **LET IT A-L-L-L COME OUT!!!**
> **TIME TO PUT OUR COLORING BOOKS AWAY…**
> **PUT OUR CRAYONS BACK IN THE BOX**
> **AND FROSTY THE SNOWMAN BACK ON THE SHELF.**

That was it, the last show—this time the station manager had tuned in, blown an abscess, and decided to pull the plug for good.

FEAR AND LOATHING IN CLAREMONT, CALIFORNIA
APRIL 1987

As Rocky Mountain rich-person hangouts go, Aspen, Colorado, is the mother lode of loaded-mother resorts. In Aspen there is no apology for the ostentatious parade of wealth; lunch will run you forty bucks; and if you're looking for the liberal-riche social and/or environmental conscience paraded about for show in similar whitey playground retreats, don't waste your time hunting too hard here. Where even Telluride frowns upon the sale of (say) hide and fur in city limits (token vestige of social lefty etiquette in the San Juan range of southwestern Colorado), Aspen can't stack enough butchered animal pelt emporiums in between Renata's Franco-Thai Bistro and Micelli's Hand-Knit Scarves twenty yards apart. No raging PETA activist am I—though I find few bones to pick in the entrails of the PETA body politik (beavers and salamanders have contributed less to the demise of the planet than homo-sapinoids). Somehow I've never managed to actually *witness*, say, a spray-paint holographic ambushing of these fashion pompous rich gop-dames from Dallas and Houston parading their full-length minks in the Santa Fe plaza on a ninety-two-degree summer day.

But man, oh, man, who could forget the time when this matronly pedigree Texan broad was prancing in the Santa Fe plaza with (you could tell) genuine cat fur down to her ankles? It's hot out, so her pageant is presumably for show. Suddenly these three creepy-crawly kids, I'm guessing they couldn't have accrued > two decades post-womb emergence, bolt from behind the cover of a cottonwood tree, their hands cemented to this oversized bucket. They scream at Mrs. Ewing, who's still swinging in fashion groove, festooned for spectacle paraded in her cat wrap—they SCREAM: **"COW BLOOD, FUR BITCH!"**

Rapidly they are upon her and in one coordinated motion they empty the pail of alluded-to-be bovine corpuscles (more likely ketchup and red dye number eight?) down this woman's neck and back. She stiffens with shock, but upon realization of what's gone down, she escalates into seizure mode—howling, yowling, and shrieking. Strangely, she is holding her head (dripping wet as well). She suddenly bends over and grasps hard at the roots of the hair on the crown of her skull. Incredibly, in one violent motion, she dislodges (what turns out to be) this garish beehive wig, dripping viscous and red, and then, on her knees, she furiously proceeds to pull it apart. Ultimately she ditches the disheveled mess, now this mucked-up wad of congealed strands and clumps, into a trashcan already filled to the top with cardboard boxes. She spits with contempt at the can, then scrambles to her feet, running in circles, once again maniacally wailing like the victim bride in *I Married a Monster from Outer Space* (the bride, you might recall, had been a good sport most of the way through what curiously turned out to be a passionless liaison with spouse; then she spots the flying saucer in the woods and hubby disembarking in zombie lockstep).

The fur-kid marauders jackrabbit away and toss the bucket of "blood" on a bench in front of the Overland Sheepskin store (ha ha). Our cow-doused matron of aristocracy shrieks for cop assistance; wigless, witless, and convulsively enraged under the cover of her red-stained lynx or jaguar or whatever, she looks more like a victim of swine flu meets Ebola (pre-Covid days).

Of the long row of old Indian women selling their jewel wares on the downtown plaza sidewalk, one in particular has been tracking the psychodrama from its incipience. She gets up and waddles over to the trash bin where the bloody wig was tossed. Her mottled, well-worn hands reach with considerable effort down, down into the trash. Eventually she latches onto the bloody, amorphous clump of fake hair. The weight of the soggy mess must have promoted its position to the very bottom of the dumpster—her shoulder is even with the top of the trash tank as her arm fully extends down with a tight grip. Quickly she emerges with the prize, shakes it a few times, and stuffs it into what appears to be a Walgreen's plastic pharmacy bag. Content, but not betraying any particular sense of accomplishment, she goes back to her spot on the sidewalk and continues hawking turquoise and onyx pendants with her colleagues. She stuffs the bag containing the afterbirth of fake hair into some sad-looking sack.

The dumpiest motel at the edge of Aspen asks $249 a night for a summer room, not even Wi-Fi'd. I was on my way to Boise, Idaho, looking forward to crashing in Rock Springs, Wyoming, the next night, ultimately setting up a day jaunt into the famed Blue Petrified Forest nearby (Rock Springs turned out to be a highway-stop scary sinkhole—avoid at all costs). So Aspen is about ten square blocks of expensive shops and fancy food emporiums with minimal charm, as boring and soulless as one would expect of a mountain playground paying homage to Beverly Hills. The specter of Hunter S. Thompson haunting this absurd circus of glitz, this glacial Riviera of Republicans and DNC daredevil donors, ambling out from the nether regions of his Owl Farm digs in Woody Creek, just a heartbeat down the road, strains credulity.

Posthumously, looking back, it may be worth a few moments of consideration to distinguish Thompson the writer from Thompson the cartoon character. Ostensibly, one might make the case that that was the point of the so-called gonzoid school of journalism, which Thompson in theory launched. This is where, it is said, the writer conjures the story or event to be reported immersed as protagonist inextricably tangled up with the cast of characters involved in the story. In Thompson's case, this often evolved backward: his escapades framed the allegory, and the ensuing exaggeration of dissolution somehow managed to depict the reality of what was to be reported in a most bemused, detached, ironic, and sometimes poignant perspective. *Fear and Loathing on the Campaign Trail*, a behind-the-scenes roller coaster ride of 1972's presidential campaign, is, once in a while, in snapshot moments, a goofball-riveting and very funny portrait of politics lobotomized. But rent the *Fear and Loathing in Las Vegas DVD* with Johnny Depp playing HST. Sorta boring, right? Sorta static, benign even, huh? The writer's gratuitous narrative as characterized in the novel is lost in the film—maybe because the damaged, drugged-out circus of events chronicled in the Sin City tome is not, by itself, that spectacularly outrageous or shocking. What's infinitely more compelling is the detached writer's persona, the confused, lost soul of the journalist attempting to separate, balance, and then account for a world that he himself has personally turned upside down. It's the irony of this kind of candid self-immolation that to this day jumps out (to me anyway) as absurd and elastically unbelievable—not the choreography of Mr. Depp performing the described anecdotes as a visual fable. The fable resides in the perspective of the writer attempting to reckon a sequence of events that he sets up and then is clueless to come to terms with.

I can only tell you that I accepted the assignment, this was back in '89, with healthy trepidation: *Resurgence of Psychedelics on College*

Gregg Turner

Campuses. That's the angle they were shopping; my editor claimed that this was, in fact, occurring. I was dubious, they were certain. And as long as I was teaching at one of these academicized magic mushroom think tanks, why not go behind the scenes, expose the blotter acid shadow students, bad trips, free-form freakouts and all? Better yet, why not dig up Owsley and Kesey, the original Svengali sugar cube chemist and the guinea pig who donated his cerebral folds to countless lysergic swathing? See what ten cents they had to offer. They were in fact on the list, but first at bat was Hunter. My editor suggested Thompson, mainly 'cause he was in the area, doing one of his storied Q and A's at a community college thirty minutes down the road. Never had thought of Hunter S. Thompson as an icon of psychedelia or even the poster boy of alternative states of consciousness in the quest of hyper dimensional realization. A gourmet of mind-bending binges and disembodied, drug-induced psychosis perhaps, but certainly not the guru of the let's-find-God groove. Still, thirty minutes was thirty minutes, and there I was, backstage at the college's auditorium, waiting to be introduced by Hunter's assistant—let's call her Olivia.

I'd been warned that he'd been salting his soul with prodigious amounts of cocaine, and in gonzo-speak "copious amounts of cocaine" might imply quantity that could fit into a washing machine or pack an entire refrigerator in one sitting. To attest to such reality, while finally mediating interview logistics with Olivia backstage at the Q and A forum, this ghostly aberration bounds out of the bathroom with what appears to be a face full of white pancake makeup. He's snorting and sniffing and licking his arms, half gyrating, wildly gesticulating like a mad, wounded animal caught in a car's high beams, but maybe more like a hooked steelhead trout fighting the line that's pulling it in. Uhm, but there were no headlights or fishing line provoking this dead-end dance. Dr. Thompson's path of orbit appeared, at that frozen instant, rather arbitrary. The pancake makeup turned out to be a patted-down, seemingly padded-down layer of coke and congealed sweat that stuck to his face after he'd apparently buried his head in... well, take a guess. Seemed to be no point asking any questions that night. Way too frantic a scene at that moment to extract insight on anything, let alone resurgent college campus bad trips. I guess.

That was Thursday night. Olivia suggested conducting the innerview Saturday afternoon—in the car on the way to Ontario Airport. I should pick them up from their hotel at lunch, she maintained, and then we jaunt to the airport, tape recorder running, HST waxing. So Friday evening is when the first of a series of unlikely phone calls clocks in at about 11:45 p.m. Olivia is concerned because "Hunter is having, uhm, a little bout with the flu." He (naturally) has a deadline first thing in the morning, and they're concerned that this nasty virus could get in the way. Do I know of, uhm, an all-night, you know, *pharmacy*, that, uh, could still be uhm, open, "You know what I'm saying?"

The funny thing is that I don't, or I didn't, 'cause I can be oblivious to a fault most of the time and clueless as a math nerd (minus the *Revenge of the...*) the rest of the time. Hence I suggested that the pharmacy at Albertson's was still open for another ten minutes, what do they need? There's a heavy silence. She's wondering if I'm playing her, no one could be that d-u-m-b not to get it, but I didn't get it, and to ratify this sad fact, I proceed to offer to drop by with a spare bottle of Ibuprofen. And now the silence grows heavy and pitiful.

"Well, look," she finally intones (now exasperated), "Hunter was wondering, since, uhm, you can relate as a fellow writer and all, understanding what it's like to meet deadlines, Hunter was hoping you could score him a little, well, you know it's not for me, strictly for Hunter, some, uhh, some cocaine?" Now I'm feeling doubly stupid. What did I expect him to ask for? High fructose corn syrup?

Ibuprofen, indeed. Still, I suppose I could make some calls. As a rule, I'm as straight as they come, not much of a druggie or drunkie, so I'm winging it here. I don't know who the hell I'd begin to phone—though I was confident that it wouldn't take many phone calls to recruit all-too-willing assistance to placate the literary legend.

So finally I rejoin with, "Well, how much is he looking for?" (Though, to be honest, I wouldn't know a snort that ranged from three grams to fourteen teaspoons.) The woman at the other end of the line tells me to hold on; she's sensing a ray of hope here. Olivia puts the phone down and the next thing I hear is this bellowing, sounds like what I'd imagine the groans of a beached whale would be, and various objects crashing to the ground.

"Uhm, Hunter would like two thousand grams."

"Okay, no problem," I respond, trying not to laugh. "Uh, thought you were gonna ask for something hard to get like perhaps fifteen pounds or whatever." I thought I was being sufficiently transparent and flip, but the person I'm talking to does not sound astonished.

She shoots back with, "Well, actually a few pounds would be great, I don't think fifteen or anything is necessary." She actually SAID this. It occurred to me that a mere 2,000 grams was a lot.

"Sorry, I don't think I can dig up the quantity he's looking for at this hour of the night (let alone anytime)." Long pause.

"Oh, I know he'll be soooo disappointed. I hope he can do the interview with you tomorrow." Well, I hope so too.

So the phone rings again at 2:50 a.m. It's Olivia once more. She's *whispering* (why?). "Hunter now accepts the fact that you cannot obtain the quantity of medicine that he was looking for, but he wants you to know that he's flexible. So he said that he'd be happy with, well, it's of course just to make deadline, he was wondering if you could perhaps get a hold of some…uh, brown, un-stepped-on Mexican heroin." Okay. I thought about this, and turned on the night-light by my bed.

"Are you kidding me, is this a joke or something?"

"Uhm, no. He really feels that this would seriously help him expedite the writing deadline he's facing and also would enable a 'killer' interview with you on the way to the airport." The thought occurred to me that perhaps this was a friend pulling my leg (just had to be, right?), yanking on my gullible underbelly, as gullible as they come, except there were only a couple of folks I knew who were aware that I was in contact with the Thompson entourage to do an interview—and they weren't very adept leg-pullers. But still.

"Well," I stammered, "I'm afraid I have no connections for anything like that, I'm sorry."

"Well, I'm sorry too. He knows you're affiliated with the engineering college, and he felt that would provide gateway to scoring something like this." Was she kidding? True, that the engineering school was the most drug-consumptive of the private consortium of colleges I was affiliated with; seems someone had been doing their homework. Nevertheless, this whole thing was more than absurd.

"Look, no can do. If he wants to talk tomorrow, fine. If not, that's fine too. Ibuprofen's still the best bet if you want anything I got. Uhm, I can crush it up for him?"

"Oh, I'm so sorry to hear that, I know that Hunter will be quite let down. He thought that for sure, I mean, if you couldn't get the coke, that this would be a more reasonable request." What a peculiar word "reasonable" is. Is it reasonable that if I buy a lottery ticket I should expect to win even five fucking dollars?

The sun comes up 6:15 a.m. and that's when the phone rings yet one more time. Oh, Jesus, what does he want now? "Two cannisters of ether," whispers Olivia. "Hunter's researched a recent story that several students at the engineering college were busted for conjuring PCP in the basement of a dorm there. He's certain that to do this, there must have been generous cuts of ether involved."

"Well, no problem. Luckily I still have my ether emergency hotline at hand," I laugh. "I'll just ring my ether contacts, and I think we're in business. You sure he only wants two?"

"Well, of course if you can produce additional amounts from your, uhh, hotline, I'm sure he'd appreciate it." I thought about this. I wish I actually had an ether hotline, whatever the hell that would involve. Sadly, I had to explain that the hotline was a spurious concocted fiction; I conceded this to Olivia, who was still whispering on the phone. "What? Oh, I know that Hunter will be extremely disappointed. Just a second, hold on." Once again, in the background, I hear this bewitched bellowing, like an impaled sea lion. Olivia returns to the phone: "I'm sorry, Hunter hopes that he is able to conduct the interview with you tomorrow; he feels he is writing on borrowed time. His words." Yeah, right.

Now it's Saturday. Promptly at noon, I arrive at the hotel and check in with the desk, in what room is the Thompson party lodged? The clerk rings the room and is told that they will call me back, hang in the lobby. So I sit, but it isn't long before a furious hotel manager accosts me. "Are you with Raoul Duke?" Uh oh.

I reply that "with," of course, is a strong label, I'm just here to conduct an interview. The manager can't control himself.

"You tell those assholes that *no one* checks into one of my rooms and installs their *own dead bolt*. You tell them that, okay?" Okay. This is already becoming more incendiary than I could have imagined. Most hotel rooms already *have* a deadbolt or second safety-lock feature. What would this mean? That an additional hole was drilled on top of all of this?

Then the lobby phone rings; I suspect it's for me. It's Olivia. Whispering again. "We will meet you at the third palm tree in the parking lot—what time do you have on your watch?"

"Uh, twelve twenty-eight."

"Okay, then let's meet up at the palm tree at twelve forty-five by your watch, alright?"

"Uhm, sure." So at 12:45 (by my watch) I'm feeling stupid, 'cause I'm standing next to a palm tree and there's no one there. 1:07, no one there. Finally, by 1:30, no sighting of life forms (gonzoid or otherwise). I look, and there, opposite the tree, is a vacant hotel room, door ajar, on the ground floor that looks like the meltdown of a small atomic detonation. What caught my attention was the door that was swinging open with the wind: there was a small circular hole (you could see through) above the card-key entrance handle. I sauntered over to the room, what to see? Empty bottles of Chivas littering the floor, trash in the sink, bloody tampons (useful for nose bleeds) strewn all over both beds and lots of typewriter paper crumpled up. All of this I collect in a big bag (that I'd borrowed from the hotel custodian)—still to this day stashed somewhere in my folks' garage.

Also on the floor in the room:

1. Half empty jar of peanut butter
2. Three empty Tropicana OJ quarts
3. Five empty packs of Dunhill cigs
4. Vaseline (small tube)
5. Box of pistachios
6. Human locks of hair (in a sandwich bag)?

So with the scheduled interview having gone south, I drove home, passed out on the bed, and snoozed for a few hours. But the phone rings again. This time it's one of my colleagues at Pitzer College. I describe in detail what transpired, but he's not buying it. "Your imagination's just too fertile," he laughs. "Better scram to your next class, tell it to them. Better yet," he laughs, "write it up and throw it in together with all the other ridiculous bullshit you tell everyone. That's what you should do." He laughed again.

Gregg Turner

Fast forward to not quite two decades later. Now it's 2005. En route to Boise Idaho. Supposed to start a one-year gig teaching the maths at Boise State University. Not at all a shameful bastion of academe, actually. I'd been fired where I'd been professing for a decade at this backwater college in Las Menudo, New Mexico. Long story. Too bloody to recount here (two years later I prevailed in a lawsuit and was hired back, granted tenure, and awarded $180,000 for egregious abuse). First stopover was Aspen. Have I mentioned that the cheapest perch in town was $249 for the night? And after I checked in, hungry as a wild dog, I settled for Renata's Franco-Thai Bistro. Two kabobs of "orange drizzle satay" and a "peppercorn crusted steak curry" with organic (of course) jasmine turmeric rice. Still hungry after the meal, $85 later, I found a McDonald's down the road a ways and had two Filet-o-fish sandwiches. Now I was in Woody Creek. Uhhh…

Something was going on. Of course I was aware HST's iconic Owl Farm layout was close at hand. But that was tomorrow's tourist trap. Now it's almost 11:00 p.m. and I manage to saunter into the famed Woody Creek Tavern. Packed with greasy-looking folks, this was much better than Renata's. Managed to score a stool in the back of the place.

He had suicided (not that night).

But I had no clue this was the eve to the next day when his ashes were to be stuffed tight in a football—well, some type of ellipsoid— and launched from some sorta home-made rocket into space. All Owl's Day. Film celebs mingled with regulars; the denizen of crusty folks packed the place in an incandescent stew of human grease. Was that Bill Murray at the bar? I didn't really give a flying eff, but obviously something was brewing. There were cops downing shots of TQ, bikers pounding beers, and two lesbians at the table next to me exchanging tongue. No kidding.

If the send-off was the next day, this was the rehearsal dinner. But I was fading fast, logged over five hours driving on a two-lane godforsaken highway from Santa Fe. Before I slipped into the nether region of zzz's at the Woody Creek Tavern (worried I'd drop down to the ground in a puddle of drool and other uncharted secretions) I staggered past comatose torsos on the pavement outside and managed to slip into my wheels and make it back to my luxury $249 Wi-Fi-less dump back in town. Grabbed a local newspaper and finally sorted out what was going on. This was one helluva wake I'd stumbled onto. Into.

Before I passed out on a lumpy mattress, my mind, in a freefall ride to oblivion, fired serotonin-fueled sinews that flashed back to the day of that ill-fated interview in Claremont eighteen years ago. Where I'd waited by a palm tree. And then collected memorabilia (that's being kind) from the unholy entrails off the floor and bathroom (I was a fan).

And then it hit me. I had to do this:

Woke up that morning, I traipsed into a CVS and picked up some tampons, Vaseline, a roll of toilet paper, and even some pistachios. Two packs of Dunhills. I cut off a few locks of curly hair above the back of my neck and I stuffed it all into a paper bag and took off pronto to Woody Creek. The little paved road that ran up past the property had some potholes and was fairly narrow. This morning, you couldn't get close. A veritable army of security blocked any chance of catching a closeup view (or encounter) of guests—so I saddled the car off the shoulder, a hundred yards from the entrance, threw it in park, and sprung out of the driver's side with the pharmacy bag of cigs, Vaseline, pistachios, roll of asswipes, and hair. I jumped onto the asphalt and started swinging the bag over my head. A handful of psychotic-looking security guards started running toward me, but before they got close, I hurled the bag across the road; it didn't matter whether it would reach the property or not, this being more of a symbolic gesture, what have you. And before the armed security cretins got anywhere near, I revved up the engine, did a quick U, and hightailed it out in the direction of Glenwood Springs down the highway.

It started to rain. Hundreds of miles to get to Boise. And I kept thinking of tanks of ether.

MAGGOTS
AUGUST 1985

And there were lots of 'em: tons of maggots. But this story really begins with two weasels. Two stuffed weasels for sale at the La Mirada (grungy Orange County, southern California) swap meet, fifteen bucks for the pair. Brother and sister? Couldn't tell. Both been shot, bullet holes badly filled in—lousy look on each of the croaked critters' mugs, but you can't blame 'em—rude end to what must have been a beautiful life. Anyhow, they were fifteen for the pair, and although my higher animally correct (AC) instincts said it was wrong, wrong, wrong (way wrong) to kill and stuff (bad stuff job) wild beasts, these guys were an impressive duo. The ol' geezer sellin' 'em was a crusty old creep who was also peddling some beat-to-shit combat boots and a couple scum-laden fruit bowls and grandma dishes with faded red rose patterns in the center for next to nada.

"You can take everything, buddy, for forty-five bucks!"

He said that without blinking, looking down at the ground, musta been a slow day—"Actually, I think I just want the weasels," I replied, fairly certain the boots and cracked dishes I could live without.

"Milton Berle once ate from these plates," that's what he said, honest; this schlock meister was pretty single-minded. But I was just as sure that I just wanted the weasels. One to put on top of the TV, the other by the blender on the kitchen sink. Maybe next time go for grandma's dishes, this moment in time we shook on fifteen GWs for the two dead balls of fur.

So now I've got these two weasels, I'm riding home—they're riding shotgun. Henry and Juan, their Christian names. Juan looked more, uhm, outraged than his brother Hank, so I imagined him glowering from over the television in this macho impressive weasel death snarl of pain and humiliation—that's what seemed to jump out, frozen in time, on his anguished, craggy little mug. Very somber—he was the poet of the two. Here's an unpublished poem of his:

The Continual Search for Food
by Juan J. Weasel

> *A ferret feels hungry*
> *A ferret feels alone sometimes*
> *A Ferret always thinks of the next time*
> *That a ferret may not find*
> *Food.*
> *Feels feels for food—wants to eat.*
> *A ferret feeds—but not all the time.*
> *Because at any moment, the "Loud Explosion"*
> *Could happen...*

Henry was more of a blue-collar weasel. He organized the Union of Worker Weasels of America (UWWA) and campaigned most of his adult life for less centralized weasel pack controls. This ultimately resulted in the Weasel Voter Reform Act of 1987, where only weasels with quarter-inch thick (or more) coats could vote in the monthly pack gatherings. Henry gained notoriety in circles of politically active weasels for the saying "you're a weasel first, a hunter-gatherer second, and a scavenger in the end."

I was thinking that Hank oughta be on the kitchen counter by the blender—or maybe by the toaster oven. No, the blender. He'd approve, I was certain of this. And by the time I got home, I was toeing the line, balancing that fine threshold of over-the-edge weasel ecstasy. Nothing could sidestep my euphoria (for at least the next hour). I began to chant out loud, "Ohhh—Hank in the kitchen, and Juan on the TV, Henry by the blender, and Juan by the remote control. Hank lookin' ripped off, Juan lookin' pissed off—both of them are weasels in my house today..." Or something as pathetic as this. It was a glorious moment. Juan looked absolutely regal. His maimed and hunched little body deflected the afternoon light cast through the green canvas curtains, dispersing seriously spooked-out shadows on the floor in front of the couch. Henry was more austere—actually, the toaster oven turned out to be the better platform. His mangled tufts of hide next to a burnt piece of bread depicted a true fighting spirit. Oh, we were all such a happy little weasel household. There was no fat, black, swollen thunderstorm in the sky to dampen our up.

But then a serious stripe of badness. Just two days after all of this, I came home from a Friday night party somewhat psychically lopsided. Not drunk or drugged, not by a longshot the type of lopsided I mean. But a couple glasses of red wine on top of what seemed to be an emerging flu—this provoked a pounding fever and a ten-minute trial to fit the key in the front door (my door?). Five minutes to find the bathroom—couldn't find. Okay, will piss in the morning. Bedroom? Crashed down on the mattress—this was around, let's say, 4:00 a.m.-ish. Sun comes up at six; eyes open and two hours of REM-deprived zzzs demand H_2O—lots of it. My tongue felt superglued to the roof of my mouth, the hell of dehydration in full swing, and seemingly no saliva anywhere to moisten. Head pounding, had forgotten to take my contacts out so by now they're sealed to both orbs with a lens-like epoxy. Need water—for mouth, for eyes, for head (forehead?)... Pain, pain was all around. Pain from inside. Pain came from deep, deep within and ushered pain from past lives. Ridiculous. Waves of pain, searing and unending, foreshadowing, no doubt, the imminent pain of eternity and Armageddon. Arm-a-gettin' sorta cold and tingly and numb all of a sudden, so—rrrrrush to the kitchen tap, watch that shaking armhand—get glass. Glass to sink. HOLD GLASS STEADY, goddamn lousy hand—Okay, that's better... Ahhh, water for mouth... Hey, for mouth, for MOUTH, not neck and pants...left handarm must help right handarm. Yeah, that's it. Ahhh, water for mouth again. More water gulp gulp gulp. Alright, enough...enough, dammit. I said, THAT's ENOUGH. STOP!!! But both hands wouldn't stop, mouth couldn't keep up. I became tattered with tepid tap water. Three glasses, four glasses—please no more... I threatened both handarms with regurgitant but they weren't impressed—four glasses of water.

I defiantly closed my mouth so that subsequent issuance of sink water failed to penetrate my now tightly sealed oral cavity. Miserable appendages, I thought. I control the brain—you're just disenfranchised paws. But suddenly, left-hand shoved its middle two fingers between defiantly clasped lips; then it used an entire fist for leverage. Mouth, now pried open painfully wide, suddenly confronted some monstrous cylinder (easily three times as large as the previous glass) filled to the brim with milky lukewarm dishwasher runoff. Oh, right hand had been busy indeed while left hand held mouth tightly ajar. The cylinder reached its target hole. And then down down down it poured the silty, slightly brown turbid concoction. Throat was appalled at the intrusion, choking and reeling. I expected to chuck in the worst convulsive way when I noticed the steak knife on the counter. I noticed it real good, and so did both handarms, quickly regrouping, only now as supple, somewhat recalcitrant players. They got the message; they understood perfectly. This was evident because the face-hole dousing ended abruptly. Still, belly was gorged and distended with vile pints of what tasted like protozoan-laced pond scum. It all had to come out—and most of it did, all over the floor. At which point handarms dropped the giant beaker that floated with a small creek of watery expectorant down and under the kitchen table. I whirled around, up and back on two hoofs weak but triumphant and seemingly back in control. Then out of the kitchen, in front of the couch, past the TV—yeah, hi, Juan—catch you later. Need to create a serious eight-hour coma here...JUAN?

Juan was larger. I don't mean in stature, or merely to the snapshot of a bloodshot sick person's eyes. Juan had...grown. Mostly (what seemed to be) his gut, he just looked fatter. Hmmm. But this wasn't the time for conflicted musings, and the concept of a dead weasel's suddenly inflated paunch could be deferred for later consideration. Bed/sleep/recovery: first order of business. So I swayed back to the bedroom and became a horizontal person without pause.

Somewhere in the afternoon, consciousness now activating the soul to life—more like a fraction of life (still reeling from whatever fanged DNA monster I'd scored the night before). I pulled myself up, quasi-vertical, and back to the kitchen for more water. Now contact lens-less, images were blurry and my focus shot to hell. But alla this matched the absence of visceral acuity in my brain and my body. More agua in the kitchen, hey Henry, what's shakin'? Uhm, (squinting) that you, Hank? Was pretty sure of this, so I pivoted around and turned on the tap once again and threw some city water on my face. Much better. Now crank the window above the sink wide open, the resulting filtered blast of fresh Southern California air and smog greedily sucked in by each wilted pore on my face and neck. I collapsed to my knees, sat down on the floor. The currents of air swept over both now un-lensed orbs. I stuck my paw in the water and swiped my face and ears one last time. The promise of consciousness and revival now greater than palpable—so I got up.

Hey, Hank, what up? "Oh, Master, I'm so happy you're feeling better," I could almost hear him squeal in his inimitable weasel's tenor. And I understood this anthropomorphic personification of goodwill to be a more than substantial indication that I was, in fact, on the road to rec(k)overy. Great—this, then, calls for extension of the afternoon Saturday nap, so back to the bedroom I trek, 'cept... Juan? Enormous Juan? Juan, what've you been eating (hunting?) while I lay comatose? Still, my severely myopic, lens-less eyeballs were unable to tighten the picture. What appeared to be a stuffed weasel's bulging belly, of course, could have been, in reality, say, (maybe?) perversely refracted rays of shade and sun. Perspective distends, relativity bends, but, before you could say "Einshtein," I was up against the television, scrutinizing the hacked and anguished mug of the critter.

This was my error: if you ever notice the tummy of your stuffed animal undulating and spent with engorged distortion, do not do this: raise the weasel over your head. Do not be impressed by the contractions and sudden abdominal animations of the stuffed, furry gut. Do not bring the weasel's vibrating torso down to within a half-inch of your eyeballs (even if that's the only way you can focus on and characterize the improbability of what's happening).

But if you *do* do all of this, if you ignore this warning and you foolishly continue to demand assessment of your bulging, writhing stuffed weasel's belly—at least DON'T DO THIS: when you hear the noise, the noise, the one that sounds like someone frantically retracting a rusted, filthy zipper down a well-worn ski parka— for GOD'S SAKE, DON'T JUST STAND THERE! And when the shower of maggots begins to spill like a tsunami wave over your head and face—CLOSE YOUR MOUTH! And many seconds later, when your brain registers that something this pitiful is, in fact, taking place—DO NOT CONTINUE TO BE PARALYZED BY THE TORRENTIAL RAINSTORM OF MAGGOTS NOW POURING DOWN THE FRONT OF YOUR PANTS, TWISTING, TURNING,

AND EXPLORING VIRTUALLY EVERY ACCESSIBLE ORIFICE AND BURROWING INTO THE FOREST OF YOUR—

because—

YOU DO NOT WANT TO RECALL, HAVE ANY LASTING MEMORY CELL IMPRINT, OF WHAT THIS FELT LIKE AND LIVE WITH THE GYRATIONS THAT SHALL LAST—to this day.

I lunged for the bathroom, I scrambled to the shower. I found a can of Drano under the sink and doused myself liberally. Fer Christ sake, fuggin' DRANO?? The showerhead's stream of no-cold, all-hot water emanating in only a light mist hardly quelled my agitation. Agitation cannot begin to rightly characterize the waves of ammonia and paralysis that now washed up against me and straightjacketed my mind. I slumped and fell down to the shower's floor. Little writhing critters by my feet now. So more Drano. More mags down the drain-o.

Eventually, I crawled pitifully slow back to the unloving living room, scene of the eruption. Juan in shreds. Juan's hide just strewn about in shards of fur on the floor, a handfulla mags still feasting on the sucker's craggy little mug and painted-red bloody ears. Tom Verlaine and then Jim Carroll were offered by the college radio station somewhere in the background. Got up, ran to check on the other weasel, the one by the blender. Blender weasel doin' just fine, but what a cryin' shame that just 50 percent of the original tag team remains.

Over the years, as much as I've tried to consecrate the apparition of the surviving weas, I've been shouted down and told to get rid of the critter, as in "now." Some folks don't like the bullet hole in the snout, some think the stuff job is not only tacky but g-r-o-o-sssss. Put the thing on top of cabinet files in my office at school one day, some spoiled brat kid complains to my department chair she was "repulsed," put off from asking any meaningful questions about the homework. Much later later later on, this gurl I was dating will only spend the night with the weasel out of sight. Apparently "outta sight" meant outta the house and in the garage. She don't wanna know about it, she don't wanna hear about it, she don't even care that it survived a maggot holocaust that eradicated the twin. So it stays in the storage shed, in the back of the garage, which is where it continues to rest amongst the dung heap of garage toss-offs that I haven't had the time to sort through for years. A dubious ending for such a regal weasel. The girl? Haven't seen her for a while now. Maybe time to drag the thing outta the shed and put it back by the blender. Relationships are tenuous things. Some weasels can last for-effin-ever. But not all.

Gregg Turner

LINDA
NOVEMBER 1995

I was planted like a sack of potatoes at the counter stool facing the downstairs bar at the Sloop John B. This was the Sloop JB before it morphed into its present tense incarnation of redneck dumbass jock bar and pool hall. Anyway, I was grading a stack of exams, swigging frugal mouthfuls of iced tea that tasted like fungoid snot-smeared socks out of the hamper—I was minding my own business, y'know?

She was perched about eight stools down, chatting it up with a girlfriend, slurping some cocktail—I mean, I couldn't tell you the difference between a Bitch on the Beach and a Shellfish On the Sand—but it looked red, so maybe it was a Cranberry Clitoris or something. She was the spitting image of a young Rosanna Arquette, early thirties. Wide blue eyes and big front teeth that on anyone else could check out more equine than attractive-human. But she was, incidentally, more than very attractive-human and more than very radiant and when she slid over, adjacent to my place at the counter, I was locked into her radar, transfixed. "Hi, I'm Linda," she offered brightly. "I couldn't help noticing how hard, uh, you were concentrating. So I thought I'd be a pest and ask."

"Grading exams. I'm an assistant professor of paleontology at Albuquerque St. University."

"Wow! What was the test about?"

"Y'know, bones," I offered casually.

"But why are you grading your exams in a bar with all this murk and noise? And it's so dingy in here!"

"I'm ADD—need the murk and intrusion of the environment, lots of noise and distraction—so I can concentrate."

"Heyyyyy," she purred, suddenly ecstatic with revelation, "I've been told I'm AT&T too!"

"Oh."

"Actually, I think it runs in our family. My son, Joshua, he's eight years old—he looks like Dennis the Menace. Ha! He makes these prank phone calls, at least I *think* that's what they are. And when I saw my last phone statement, I almost passed out."

"Sounds like quite a kid."

"Oh, he's great. I mean, one time he dialed up a 900 psychic-hotline number and he looked pretty confused after that—I'm not sure what they told him."

"Maybe that good ol' Mr. Wilson said hi."

"Yeah, that's cute." (She obviously didn't think so.) She persisted: "You know what the funny thing is? Well, since that night, I've become sorta hooked on the psychic hotline scene myself." She smiled, only feigning embarrassment. "You know what this woman, she sounded like she was from Brooklyn, told me last night?"

"No, what?"

"That I'd be meeting someone soon."

"A business meeting?" I wasn't clear where she was going with alla this; intent and context have always worn an opaque sheen to my interpretive tentacles, particularly when it comes to picking up or tuning into signals.

"Silly!—like a romantic rendezvous—and it's supposed to happen tonight! Can you believe it?!"

Gregg Turner

I put down my pen and stopped tallying the test scores. "Tonight? So, what, are you just hanging around, waiting for this to happen?"

"Welllllll—I think it's just *starting* to happen, do you see what I'm saying?" She put her hand on my shoulder and looked into my eyes. "Are you seeing anybody?"

"Uhm," I was thrown off guard, "it's sorta dark in here, otherwise I could probably pick up the folks on the other end of the counter. I'm just getting shadows, some, uh, hazy outlines, is that what you mean?"

She started laughing. "Jesus, you really crack me up. You're pretty damn funny, Dr. Dermatologist."

And I joined in her chorus of cackles, still not 100 percent clear what we were laughing about. "That's *paleontologist*—bones, not SKIN."

"Whatever! Hey, but aren't the bones *under* the skin?"

Before I could respond to this, she put her left hand gently over my mouth and rested it there. "Shhhhh, you think too much." She sucked on the tip of her right middle finger for a few seconds, then inserted it into my mouth between the middle and index fingers of her left hand still covering my face.

Cherry! It was a cherry-flavored finger! Not pomegranate or star fruit, just maybe bing cherry. With this epiphany, I conceded to our psychic-hotline fate. The conceit of being hunted by a beautiful and very funny/klutzy (even pretty damn intelligent—she'd been slaving away at a pulp novel!) apparition like Linda proved too much to ignore. And over the course of several months, we maintained a pretty close liaison, though the stability and longevity of where this was all heading was always and continuously precarious. Edgy. She had a few, oh, let's call them, quirks. She liked, how should I put this, dug the most: lime Jell-O. I'd heard stories of how she'd fill the bathtub with the stuff. And I call this a quirk because she apparently did not like the TASTE of lime Jell-O—just the odor and the color. One night, I prepared a special dessert—I'm literally talking after-dinner dessert here, in case your mind's wandering into uncharted territory (don't go there). She cooked chicken, and I prepared what I thought was bound to be a hit: green Jell-O with French vanilla ice cream and fig pieces. But when I brought it out, she went berserk. "Fuck you!" she screamed and took off to the bedroom, loud bang and click (door shut and locked). See, there was that kind of volatility to the relationship (was it in fact an R-ship? I could never be certain).

Her kid was a brat, sorta, maybe no more of a brat than any kid is these days and he was quite bright, especially adept at manipulating mom's attention. It was more than once when he'd pound on the bedroom door at 2:00 a.m. craving attention when mom was busy. And there was Shame. Shame was the default playmate for Joshua, he lived next door, he was nine years old. But he was a smart-ass, and creepy as all fuck—like a prepubescent Eddie Haskell. I was never clear whether Shame was the legal moniker or an appointed nickname for reasons I chose to ignore. Shame would invariably steal Josh's toys or stomp on the most treasured of the kid's possessions, a bag of McDonald's French fries. Then there was the time he dumped a handful of spiders down Josh's pants—one of the arachnids apparently fanged the poor kid's highly allergic appendage and it swelled up to a semi-hideous dimension (Joshua wouldn't go out of the house for a week 'cause Shame and the trashy little girl from across the street, Natalya, would taunt him with "Spiderman, Spiderman, Spiderman"). Shame was a punk, and his daddy was an auto-mechanic who thought he could play the blues. The high watermark of this idiot's life occurred when he was allowed to sit in at the Horse and Cowhand Saloon one night. Jammed a couple twelve-bars and proved that he was no worse than any of the other dreadful blues fossils that were jammin' with him. Shame had a lot

Gregg Turner

of anger issues because the mechanic dad often worked over the son just like the way he would a highway-wrecked Toyota. Well, y'need to start feelin' the blues from *somewhere* I guess.

Shame would spy on Linda outside her bedroom window and tell everybody about the obsessions she had, rituals he couldn't fully understand. Nobody believed him 'cause previously he claimed to have witnessed all sorts of outrageousness (like the time he saw Linda lying on the floor with more than modest bondage gear on, or the time Linda's pooch Hoover got a little carried away with her feet when she was nodding out on the bed). He told his dad about the late-at-night, crazy-assed shit he'd seen and the dad knocked him around for "talkin' filthy crap" about people. Two days later, the dad rapped on Linda's door with flowers and a gee-tar. Wanted t'know if she'd like to hear some blues. She said no.

We were a unit, albeit an inconsistent one, me, Linda, Josh, and Hoover, allowing for the above eccentricities. Still, the evening of October 30 caught me by surprise. I was sitting in my office at school grading a last batch of midterms, and it was close to midnight. Phone rings, it's Linda. "Come over, I have a surprise for you."

"A *what*?"

"A surprise—a real, real, real BIG surprise!"

"Linda, I have to get through these scores tonight, how about later on—or tomorrow?"

"GODDAMMIT—your surprise is HERE—right fucking now!"

"Well, it'll take me about forty-five minutes to get back to town."

"Heyyyy—just do it! You won't be sorry!" Then sweetly, "Pleeeeeze." I pictured her contagious satellite smile, so enchanting and lovely; I was really helpless.

So at around one a.m., I pulled up, found a space in the Full Moon Apartments parking complex, and, with more than a bit of trepidation, got out and ambled off to her door. Knock knock. "That better be you," she screeched on some splintered high.

"No, actually, it's the blues dork down the hall."

The door swung open, she yanked my arm, and I catapulted into the living room.

"Surprise, sweetheart!"

She was decked out in a black leather corset, shiny leather boots, and black vinyl panties and swatting herself with a riding crop. Her eyes were opened wide, I mean W-I-D-E. And she was hyperventilating. This was all a bit comical, trick or treat, 'cause this was, in fact, Halloween eve, y'know? But apparently there was no theme intended for the concept.

"We've been seeing each other for almost six months now, and I figured it was about time to share something with you—something that's very important to me."

"Uh, okay." I had no idea where this was going.

She grabbed me, locked my arm with hers, and dragged me into the bedroom. Door slams shut, dead bolt on door, "whap," locks tight. She pushes me up against the wall. She is salivating. Her eyes are still wide open, half-crazed, half imploring me to "understand." I started to laugh—it was too silly and at the same time too seemingly serious. She slapped me across the side of the face, which quickly turned bright red. Then she sunk her front incisors into my upper lip, forceful enough to draw small spots of blood. She squeezed the wound and wiped the wet crimson beads on her face.

"You can laugh again, if you'd like..." She seemed satisfied with whatever point she'd felt was made. I declined to laugh. There was pathology here—and I think I leaked a few drops of recalcitrant pee in my pants. What a wuss.

"I haven't been able to describe to you the type of PAIN that I need that really turns me on." She was intense with this message; it was clear that I was about to be initiated into a parallel universe. "I'm not talking about some stupid bondage foo-foo crap, y'know what I'm saying? I'm talking about how you can take me into another realm, another dimension. Take me to a place where I can climax outside of my body."

"Linda, I..."

"Shut up—just listen to me. I want to know—are you man enough to send me to this place? I want to go to Mars, dammit, and I need to know if you have the rocket ship and the brutality to take me there?"

I was troubled by all of this. Jell-O was one thing, but delivering copious amounts of "PAIN" was another. Why does this always fucking happen to me? I mean, I was with Laurie Goldstein for over a year when she confessed that her "stuffed animal sex toy habit" was "out of control." And after three months with Lisa Stewart, I found out she wasn't a paralegal at all—just a dancer at Hal's Body Shop. Why, even Annie Moskowitz, after two years, admitted that she wasn't really a vegetarian. Just around *me*! What's that about? And finally we have "PAIN." PAIN seemed the place to draw the line. Instinctively, I unfastened the boudoir deadbolt, jarred open the door, and hurled myself into the hallway.

"Mommy, what's going on?" Joshua had been snug in his bedroom, not too thrilled about the circus playin' out outside of his door, but he was now threatening to emerge. More than ever, this was all way too loopy for me, evacuation suddenly the plan. But the front door was bolted shut and would not open. Linda was shrieking from her room: "YOU LOWLIFE CREEP, GET BACK HERE, YOU CAN'T GET OUT!" My heart started to race. I ran for the window but it was fastened shut as well. I pounded on the frame holding the glass, hoping desperately to jar something loose—loose enough to pry open and hurl myself outside. But, ugh, not getting anywhere.

"Mommy, Mommy, I want to come out now." You can call Linda crazy, but you can never accuse her of being an uncaring mother. She unlocked the kid's door (still decked out like she was a stand-in from Russ Meyers's "Faster Pussycat Kill Kill"), and while she negotiated a motherly chat to calm Joshua, I figured it was now or never. I was ready to lunge through the glass— but suddenly the window, it slid open. Like magic. Instead of shattering the night air with shards of sharpness, I tumbled most seriously out into the bushes three feet below. A ghost? Telepathy? A guardian angel? Naw, just Shame. He'd seen this all before. What a guy!

I darted to my car, slammed it into gear, and made tracks down Saint Swithin's Drive under the canopy of a two-thirds lunar haze and what seemed like galaxies of glistening stars.

Linda and I haven't spent much time together since that manic night. Still, I think of her all the time. She really had this soft, malignant radiance. A virtue that was so sweet, unusual and encouraging, plus or minus the, uhm, eccentricities. Her wit could eviscerate a fox and at the same time charm a koala! If I bumped into her tomorrow I'd not so reluctantly let her know how much I miss her.

Ultimately, we remain friends. We talk on the phone once in a while and pretend like that evening never existed. She says she's not seeing anyone these days, but I couldn't help but notice her sitting there—last week, in a booth, at Denny's with Shame's pa. She beamed and exuded an aura of satisfaction, and there was a gleam of peace and completeness about her that I'd never witnessed. And the pa, boy, he had strong forearms with a hairy gorilla tattoo on one of 'em. Had his gee-tar by the booth, just in case someone might saunter by and request some o' that thar fancy bluegrass and blues. But as far as I can tell, don't think he had any takers. Thank god.

NO MORE DOG
OCTOBER 1982

Henry "Hank" Jones was losing it bigtime when he finally *erupted*—transported to some gnarled-out peak of frenzy, he was infused with an adolescent promise of manic expectation in his veins that, in turn, coerced a wellspring of blood opiates to bust through the gates of his weary brain; this mixture combined, swirling like a furious whirlpool behind suddenly bulging eyes. "Hey, man," he shrieked, fever-pitched to the phone, "check it out!"

One eye opened, I looked at my watch. It was some ungodly hour of the morning, maybe nine thirty. Pried open another droopy orb, took a swig of semi-warm 7UP from the cup on the counter by the bed, and slid the telephone receiver snug between my ear and a lumpy pillow.

"Hank? What's...uhhh...the problem?"

"Man, you won't believe it," he cackled. He was riveted on some weird, amped-up frequency, and I knew better than to try and brake the buzz—much better option to let the inertial surge ride itself out. But what were we riding here? Jones up with the sun? This guy doesn't take the night-mask off before *noon*. "In the *Recycler*," he gasped, then exploded with certainty: "The DOGS!"

"Like in *woof*?"

"Like in *major* woof, man. Like a goddman *pack* of woofs! Listen to this..."

But before I could listen to anything there was a loud cr-rash that blasted my eardrum halfway to hell and back. "Fucking *shit*," *I* was the one screaming now, wrestling the phone away, right ear reeling from pulverized auditory nerve-endings. And then I could hear him shrieking. And ranting. And raving—like you would from a blood-soaked orgasm or something.

"You there, you still there?"

"Jones, what the hell's going on? What *was* all that?"

"Hey—never mind. It's okay. But dig *this*, man:

'Hybrid wolf pups. 1/2 Husky, large-boned. Big paws, papers. $400 each. See to believe. 555-6775.'"

Uh oh. Back page dog ads again. A big, fenced yard, with no hound to bound about and mash its affection-starved fangs on his curly black locks—the drive for unrequited dog love apparently had again assumed center stage. I mean, we'd been dog hunting before, but these days he cruises the canine classifieds with a vengeance and an ugly gleam.

Black Show Poodle? ["No way, man."]

AKC Dachsund? ["No hotdogs."]

A Lab from the pound? ["Too friendly."]

Too *friendly*? Okay, how about a pissed-off Pit Bull, its anthro-anguished dog-drool seeping from seething, swollen jaws, projectile frothing like the arc of spew from a high-pressure firehose? ["Number four in the animal kingdom in pounds per square inch of jaw pressure," he notes dutifully]. Or maybe a fang-ready Rottie mongering for mailperson fresh flesh and assorted corpuscles and spleen? ["Better."] Then why not just load a can of centipedes and toss 'em in someone's hair? No, this was the point: a killer dog is a killer dog is a potentially killer anything, pet or organism—but, after all, the lure of the cold-nosed critter was, stripped of sharp teeth and claws, for *compassion* and some serious dog bonding—lots of late-night licks and paw games and role reversing and so forth and so on. But lose the cheeseball mutts, the wussy priss-hounds of fluff and hair, diva spaniels, or tub-of-lard bassets. And you can factor out the felines—he'd rather commune with ick-ridden goldfish.

Still "woofoids" (hybrid lupus) might just work. Why not? The concept, man in search of beast (but, in this case, more like *beast* in search of beast), was evident. "They see color, think human," he hissed, suddenly more enthusiastic than six seconds before, "and mark territory well."

"Yeah, well, so do goats…" I wasn't sure whether this was, in fact, the case, but it seemed a reasonable assertion and, if nothing else, *tactical.* The nonstop canine coercion was quickly losing its luster. Now my *left* ear, pasted to the phone, was sore and there was this bladder situation that was beginning to be a problem—time to mark some mean territory myself.

But he wouldn't let go. "Listen, man. I got my mom's Beemer— why don't we make a day out of it? I think the lupine scene's happening. And, uh, what's that Sally chick up to today? Bet *she'd* wanna do the dog thing with us, don't you think?"

Ohhhh, Christ. I *knew* it. Here we go with that Sally stuff again. How could I have guessed *this* was gonna worm its way outta the goddamn psychic woodwork? It was two weeks ago, waiting for the doors to open at some off-the-mark punkabilly-rock show in Duarte. Close friend of mine, Sally Ann Silver, eldest of the three Silver sisters, was standing in line when Jones sauntered by and (his description) "caught her aura." Not the cosmic aura you catch from stray psychic forces or occult projections. Or the quasi-cosmic aura from which you awake with radical REM vibes during the night. Or even a *pseudo*-aura or a short-lasting aura*ette.* But the *other* kind— the *animal* type that you intercept from not-stray sex-scenting. It comes from the pubic and armpit hair—and, like strong ammonia, can rapidly overpower sensitized receptor-antennae for those tuned to the right channel. Was Henry Jones tuned "to the right channel"? Did it matter? Probably not.

"Pointed my way," he was sure of this. Of the direction of the hormonal vector field aimed at his heart. Cupid's stupid arrow fires, he falls, sure he has slept with "the scent" that night—and many other nights as well [and scents?]. And so this Sally business creeps into the creepy mainstay of thought more or less each time we speak. But now comes round twenty-three, "Maybe, don't you think, Sally wants to go dogging [sic] *with* us?"—he hadn't tried this angle yet. Surely the carrot at the end of the proverbial stick (if you'll pardon the metaphor) now reveals itself in the form of—are you ready?—communion with the beast! Well, *small* beasts with little pink tongues and big, black, cold noses, but— he's thinking—I *know* he's thinking—actually, we're both thinking, how could *anyone* pass this kind of entertainment opportunity by?

Still, this whole Sally thing was an affliction. A miserable obsession and a severely bad sign (for me) that he's yelping for tall, blonde Sal to join in the puppy party.

So I play it vacant: "You talkin' about...?"

"C'mon, you know who I mean. The one who digs me."

"She likes your hair."

"She digs me, man."

"Well, it's not like—or where she can't sleep at night or anything."

"Hey, y'know. Chicks are always that way. Besides, when it's crunch time...I'll bet..."

"Yeah, right, Hank. Look, what's goin' on today, you wanna make the four-paw thing a reality or what?"

"Let's unify." He was suddenly focused. "We meet up with Sally— and then make the dog rounds. Can you visualize this event? God, she's gonna be a giant hormonal nerve-ending by the time we're done. Oh, man, when I drop my head and the mutts start tugging..."

"Oh, yeah, that'll do it every time... Okay, okay, I'll try her number [*thinking*: she'll forgive me in a year or two or six]—and see what's up. Maybe we all can get together first at the Cold Girl Grill in BH, that's near you, right? But I think her pal Melanie's in town. Is this going to interfere with your animal business?"

"What? No way, it'll be like a giant dog show—*with women*!"

"Yeah...right... Uhh, look, Hank, say at about one? At the Cold Girl?"

"The *coldest*! See you there, man."

Somewhere by the beach, sometime past the stroke of noon, Sally Silver kicks a blue bug VW coupe into gear, best-pal Melanie "Mel" Bailey riding shotgun, and launches out across the choked-off span of streetways on the west end of the city. Scamming canines wasn't at the top of her shopping list as far as priority things to do— or even up there with ways to kill time on a slow Saturday. But this Hank Jones cat, he was like a trip and a half. Played stand-up bass and sang for some retro punkabilly combo called Hank Jones and the Sore Losers. But it was more like a wavelength of weird religion to the guy. He lived and breathed the shit. Collected all the impossible-to-find records, scoured the unheard-of B-sides, charted the chords, slept with the lyrics, and readjusted the attitude. *The Cool and the Crazy*, that cheesy celluloid mosaic of backwash fifties counter-culture? Well, that was the blueprint. Beatnik bongos, coiffed hairtops, wrap-around shades, and ultra-spaced-out vibes cavorting to the throbbing pulse of the two-chord Neanderthal riff. Caveman fifties (think Corman's "Bucket of Blood") meets the swinging sixties. Stomp, stomp, stomp, plus or minus the sixties hallucinogenic transmission, 'cause—to be honest—Jones's vibes were never really all that hallucinatory. In fact, doubly honest, Hank wasn't a huge fan of altered states or any type of extraneous stimulation for that matter: pot or peyote, wine or nicotine. Just the bongo beat! All that mattered. No sixties free love crap either. Love never traveled all that freely in the paths of orbit Henry Jones navigated, not that my paths were anything to write home about either.

Nonetheless, Sally furrowed her brow and projected trance-like, locked onto visions of debauched sexual mutation. She pictured "mutant" encounters and recurrent episodes involving "wet hair"—hair, hair, hair, she just couldn't lose the visual fix. It fired her rockets, but was deeply disturbing and repulsive at the same time. She conjured pictures of a towering thicket of thick, matted fur covering the entire frame of some guy's shoulders, down the spine and lower back. Like, you couldn't see back-flesh, skin of any kind under it. She could feel her blood racing at the thought of losing her hand down it. Maybe she might find a bug. As her mind and pulse coursed furiously now, she continued to bathe in this brain-ride to oblivion. She recalled the story of the homeless man in a trashy tabloid, he was known as "Daddy," and he was arrested, snatched by the cops from some lewd party involving midnight weirdness of high-decibel frenzy. Daddy's hoary harem of womenfolk were instructed to comb and tidy the unkempt and flying tufts of sweating, hairy hide down Daddy's backside and hind! Then it's movie time: sheep screwing cows and something about a slaughterhouse and two old men with lice-infested beards and mud wrestlers with long black braids swatting the moistened... Uhh, well, and then there was this thing about the pizza delivery guy: double cheese and sauce, that's what's ordered, but it comes in the box smothered under a...reddish...wig. A wig? A *WIG*? *MORE HAIR*?!

WHOAH! Sally jammed on the gas, grooving onto a track of asphalt that headed into Beverly Hills. The neurotransmitters in her mind were flying fast, furry, and furious, and the rush of this self-induced frightmare seemed just too compelling to let go of. Hard to figure what was real and what was Memorex, all these crazy stories about the guy, but then what if he starts breathing heavy at the restaurant? And what about this "me and you, we hunt dogs together today" wild card? Yeah, what *about* it? She contemplated this, smiling thinly at Mel as they pulled over to park, still zoned out with appalling daydreams and uncharted possibilities.

"Sal, what's the deal? You're zombie-ing."

"Oh, it's nothing. I guess I'm hungrier than I thought."

"You still bummed 'cause Allen didn't return your call last night?"

"No way, that schmuck's a real pain in the ass. I lucked out—now I'm off the fucking hook, y'know?"

"Uh huh...what about this one—this Jones guy? I hear he heats up pretty quick when he hears your name!"

"Jesus, Mel, what side of the bed did *you* wake up on? Besides, I don't really even know him very well. I've seen his band play—they're pretty hot for the stuff they do, that Cramps-like rockabilly stuff, y'know. But I've talked to the guy a couple of times—I don't know what his problem is. But...I think there *is* one, though...somewhere."

"Is one *what*?

"A problem. A real big one."

"A real *big* one, eh?"

"Oh, right, that's really funny. I think I'm getting ill."

But they both laughed at this, Mel crinkling her nose in the process.

"Is he cute?"

"Sure. Like, he's got this untamed way about him—I mean, that doesn't really bother me one way or the other—but there's all these really crazy stories going around. He's a hot dude, looks pretty wild... I mean, what're we fucking *talking* about? We're gonna have lunch now—not foreplay." Mel giggled and got out of the car, Sal slammed her door shut, and they both crossed the street and walked through the dark wood doors of the Cold Girl Grill.

Jones was nervously pacing by the counter in the back. He was hungry. Hungry for lunch, hungry for dogs, and hungry hungry

hungry for tall blond Sally Silver. "I haven't had pancakes in a while," he thought, trying to quiet this agitation, "but, like, they do Belgian Waffles here better than almost anyone." It was a tough call—he nabbed a menu off the counter and the pacing picked up. "God, when are those two chicks gonna get here?"

"Hey, Hank? You back there?" I'd just tromped in and spotted this particularly furtive-looking shadow in the back by the bathrooms, alternately pacing, hulking, and hunkering down. Must be him. From the looks of things, he seemed as wigged as the disembodied voice on the phone that morning.

He looked up, "What'ya think about waffles?"

"Hank?" He was *really* frayed. Hadn't seen the guy this worked up since the time he found a copy of *Wolfman Takes Two Brides* to rent at the specialty video place he logs long hours. "I was asking...about waffles," he muttered, this time more withdrawn and slightly uncentered.

"Uhm, well, yeah—I'm always up for a good waffle. What's the deal? You okay? Hey—Sal and Melanie are hangin' out in front. We should probably, uh, get realized here and then go over and say hello...or something... Don't you think?"

"I'm ready." He wiped his forehead with a quick swipe of a fist and bounded off to the table.

"Is that the guy?" gasped Melanie Bailey. He was quite a sight pouncing through the place, the rock-dude wave of curled black hair flopping up and down wildly on the top of his head—in synch with a cluster of veritable 2.5 seismic events that each long and sloppy stride of thigh, calf, and hoof seemed to generate.

"Oh, my god," leered Sal under here breath. "I *think* so." In fact, she *knew* so, but the point was moot. Anyway, if Allen had called back, she probably wouldn't even be here. But life's short and he can go to fucking hell.

"Hi, girls! Sal, you look radiant!"

"Thanks, Hank, you, uhm, sort of do too."

He wiped more sweat, now profusely dripping down his suddenly beet-red-to-maroon face, and smiled broadly. Hey, this was gonna be alright.

"Did I ever tell you the joke about the army captain," he looked around suspiciously, then added, "who had five wives? Each one..."

I interrupted quickly: "So what time is our dog appointment?" Jones let go of the punch line, possibly grateful for the opportunity to do so, then sported something about how we have an hour or so to eat—then "go dogging." So we quickly devoured the food, waffles and all, eager to dog. Hank kept brushing his foot against what he thought was Sally's ankle—it turned out to be one of the legs of the old oak table we were seated at.

"I've often thought that a dog's eyes are the real windows of the soul," he suddenly intoned. "Our soul, their soul, the soul of being, of breathing. Of fucking life and death—if we could just read into the vitriol behind the orbs, we'd begin to unravel the mystery. We'd understand infinity. We'd no longer be afraid."

I chimed in: "Our moments alive would be realized on the wall of a puppy's retina. Think about it."

Mel looked up at both of us: "You guys, you're like dog retards, is that it?"

But she said this with a smile, so we all smiled too, and Jonesy, hyperventilating in the weak hope that this was not meant in earnest, offered a sacrificial grin. He scratched above his ear, an annoying reflex that betrayed sudden angst, perhaps appalled at the possibility our insightful dog theories of the infinite had been rudely rejected and dismissed as the ramblings of...uh..."dog retards."

"Well, when we get to the dogs," Sally sensed the open wounds, "you can fill us in with greater detail."

And he beamed appreciatively for the handout—and returned the serve: "You bet!"

Eventually we all piled into Jones's mom's blue BMW, off and running to dig the hybrid lupus reality, Sal and Melanie backseating it; I rode shotgun. The tires screeched, the car lurched out into the road, and we made some serious tracks into the San Fernando Valley. He kept looking into the rearview mirror to catch Sally's eye, but she wasn't buying it.

"Unlike most canines, wolves see in color."

"Great," she said.

He opened his eyes wide, just like the humanoid-space alien dude played by Paul Birch in the original Roger Corman classic *Not of This Earth* ["Luke into my eyees, they are aaaa-lien," Birch would sneer in this crypto Armenian-like accent to unsuspecting earth victims unfortunate enough to have luked into his eyees]. He tried again to rearview Sal, eyeballs and brows straining as if to force the connection. But he locked with Mel instead. She quickly looked out the side window, the sandwich just swallowed now threatening to launch up her esophagus. There was something intensely creepy about all of this; she could feel it; it was more than palpable. She wished she was back near the beach. God, a mocha latte sounded great too. How'd she get trapped into this? Why does she so readily acquiesce to doing stuff she doesn't wanna do in the first place? But maybe it'll be a hoot! Maybe these guys're gonna get Sal to march around on her hands and knees with him. They can sniff each other and chase tennis balls. She cackled silently; passive-aggressive projection was the only trick working right now; she felt cranky and cornered, her disposition doing alternate 180s. Mood is a funny thing: it's so context driven!

"Mel, I'm especially delighted you could make it." He was still trying the eye thing for Sally in the mirror, so this rather hideous expression seemed to be frozen on his kisser. "We'll be there soon. It's always tense anticipating." Was he reading her mind? Why couldn't

Gregg Turner

she just be invisible? "I think you'll get a kick when we greet the pack. These are gonna be *big* ones—hey, you have really nice, soft auburn-blonde hair. Is that your real color?"

"Uhmmm," she didn't wanna talk about her hair. She was starting to hate the concept of hair.

"Oh, Melanie," he persisted, "I was wondering about…"

She tried to deflect: "Well, the roots…actually, Sal's is the genuine thing. We, uhm, were fooling around the other day with…and Sal kept saying how you were grokking on her hair color that night you guys met…and…" She looked down at her feet—a softball serve for the guy to take the bait. She nervously glanced at Sally. Tag, you're it. Hank was jacked with anticipation at the opportunity to reengage Sal.

"Why, I was being profuse that night, Sally, but I hadn't realized that it registered so profoundly. Okay—I'm flattered!" He beamed, suddenly a newfound enthusednik. And the rush of flattered endorphins allowed increased blood flow to his foot, the one on the accelerator—and off we went. Sal glared heavily at best pal Mel, and then, whoooosh! On to the San Diego Freeway, up over the Sepulveda Pass—Sepulveda-passing lightweight Colts and Hondas at seventy-five miles per hour. "What a glorious day to be driving. It won't be long now."

And it wasn't: the seconds flew by, and minutes were created—but not more than fifteen or so of these, and we were off at Reseda Boulevard out in the west reaches of the Valley.

9244 Reseda Boulevard was the wrong address, but it was the one we had. That was my fault. The true coordinates were 9422, but in a dyslexic-move-of-the-month, I scrawled 9244.

And 9244 was a Chinese food place, Szechuan I think. But no one had any reason to believe that Szechuan wouldn't have dogs. Well, they did—or at least they, uhm, *used to.*

We walked in, waiter guy comes over to seat us, but Hank's ahead of him: "Hey, bro, are the dogs here—the ones in the paper?"

"You want *dog*?" the guy asks in disbelief.

"Dog, like the…dogs—in the ad—in the paper," says Jones, sure that the extra emphasis oughta clarify.

"NO DOG!! NO MORE DOG! THREE WEEK AGO, DOG. *BUT NO MORE DOG NOW.*"

"No, look," says Henry, now quite hyper; how to make this guy understand. "Not a dog, but dogsssSSs. Ad in the paper—for dogsssSSs."

Waiter fellow starts checking us all out, can't figure why we don't get it—no more dog. Sal and Mel're staring at the ground again—they seem to think they get *something* that we, Henry and I, don't. And to whatever thought they dialed, it wasn't brightening up their day.

[Mel thinking:] "Fucking *gross*, they do dogs at this place."

[Sal thinking:] "Why the hell didn't we stay home? Shit."

[Hank thinking:] "How to make this guy understand…?"

"Where's the manager?" I ask feebly. "We're, uhm, not making headway here."

So manager person comes out—this big guy with a white chef's hat and waist apron—and he's holding a big, big, shiny meat cleaver.

And he says, "What you want?"

"Want dogs," Hank spits out reflexively, but Meat Cleaver looks my way and I say, "Uhh, sir, we were responding to the ad in the newspaper about the wolf-hybrid puppies."

"PUPPIES?! What you think is, PET STORE?"

He smirked, then cackled a bit, apparently amused with himself. He had two gold-capped incisors. And his hand clutched the cleaver tighter and closer to his waist.

"No, look…" I thought to wax monosyllabic; maybe he doesn't process the Anglais: "puppp—peeees. In a bassss—ketttt, maybe? In baaackkkkk?" Lots of people sell their mutts from their business— maybe this guy didn't place the ad. Maybe the dishwasher's selling.

"PUPP—PEEES?! IN BAAACKKK??NEVER PUPP—PEEEES,

ALWAYS MALE ADULT! ONE **TIME ONLY!!**

BAASSS—KETTT IN BACK??

ALWAYS IN FREEZER, WHAT YOU THINKING???

WITH HEAD OFF—BUT NEVER AGAIN DOG, TOLD MAN THREE WEEK AGO, DOG ONLY ONCE. AND NO PUPPP—PEEES—IN...BAAAACK.

NEVER PUPP—PEEES.

HA HAH HAH HAH HA HA HA..."

He turned around and walked back to what looked to be the kitchen. He was laughing convulsively as his voice trailed off: "NO Pupp-peeees. NO puppp—peees in baaaack. Ha ha ha ha...No pupp—peeeeeees. No puppp—peeess...Not in baaa...aa cck! Never pupp—peeess ha ha ha ha, no pupp—peees ," and so forth.

Two Days Later

I tapped out a rhythm on Henry's front door. He'd been bummed from the chopstick canine fiasco. Only last night he called me up, told me there was something special to show me. Come over tomorrow, but not before noon.

It was raining pretty hard now, and sidewalk steam from the wet pellets bouncing off the hot summer pavement elevated into a dank mist like some half-assed fog machine from a heavy metal show. Frankly, I was more than ambivalent about stepping into chez Jones. What the hell was so important anyway? Maybe it was the ozone from the weather, or just the cumulative din from all the car exhaust and humidity seeping through the clammy gray mist, but the damp, turgid vibe in the air had me bounding through his front door before I was invited. "Hey, Jones, you here?" Where the fug was he? Front door actually led into the kitchen, where there were scraps of chicken and rice all over the sink. The fridge was open, and a beat-to-shit box of Sugar Frosted Flakes had found perch on an unlit burner over the stove. I heard a muffled groan from a couple rooms down, so I bounded through the hall and finally craned my head through the cracked door in his bedroom.

He was snoring with two towels draped over his butt. The Zorro-with-the-eyeholes-taped-over night mask insulated his orbs from the intrusion of noonday sun—it was about one thirty in the afternoon now; left unmolested he wakes in an hour or two. But I didn't have that kinda time, so I nudged the cloth on his hind and tugged gently at Zorro. He groaned, pretty tranqued out and heavy with morning sleep, attempting to wiggle deeper into his coma. So I played tough guy and took my ignition key and slipped it into his right nostril about, oh, a quarter of an inch. But that's all it took, 'cause he bounded to life, grabbed the butt towels now on the floor, and ran to the bathroom.

"Hey, I'll be with you in a minute," he bellowed. "You won't believe this when I show you." I heard the sink running, and I wasn't sure if I wanted to wait in his room, so I ambled out to the couch out in the den, and just as I plopped down on a leather sofa, he was ready to go. I mean in warp drive. He'd thrown on his Rocky and Bullwinkle T-shirt and sweats and now frantically reached into a drawer where he produced some unlabeled, black, encased video.

"I want to have a party. I want to invite those two nutty broads, Sally and what's 'er name... And we'll watch videos."

"Uh, yeah, but..."

"No buts," he admonished. "Now, look, I dug the most of the glimmer of hungry yearning from too-tall-Sal when I was ready to merge with the pooches. At the same time, when the woof pup show crashed and burned, I was grooving to the obituary ads, you know what I'm saying, like the only place to go after that fiasco was a support group meeting of the hemlock society." I nodded, unsure

Gregg Turner

of the evolution. "So...I mean, I was ready to go upside down and let my Elvis locks droop down into the pups' lair. Remember when those Rednecked Coon Healers—I think there were three of 'em last September—remember when they just grabbed hold and started tugging, and then they were just fucking *hanging by the strands of all the hairs on my head?*"

I wasn't sure that I was proud to recall any of this, but what was the point?

"Well, I've been thinking. Did you see how jazzed Miss Sally chick was getting the more I talked about the hair and dog show?" I didn't see it this way, but I let him go on. "Oh, man, dial upper-case O for 'orgasmotronic!' If that Szechuan joint had the hounds, I would have unraveled my dog trick, and man, she was ready to patty melt on my rye bread, you know what I'm sayin'?"

The image was grotesquely gag-able. "Hank, listen..."

"No, no—no, hear me out." His eyes were wet with his own anticipation. "Here's the thing—I've got all this stuff, uhm, y'know, these tapes, I just got a really good print of *The Pig Farmer's Daughter*—a real barn-burner, ha, ha—and some, uhmm, devices and things like that, y'know, like in my closet...and I was thinking, if she goes for the dog show, then she'll REALLY get off when she sees..."

"When she sees...?"

"Huh?"

"When she sees...WHAT, Hank? Whatcha gonna show her from the big bad closet? A monkey mask?"

"Heyyyy—that's pretty good, don't got none of those around, wish I did, man. But...something even better..."

He bounded up and outta the room, and I could hear the symphony of the strides down the hall mushroom their intensity. There was a discernible BANG, something crashing down— actually, a bunch of crap sounded like it was cascading down from a high shelf...lots of commotion. Finally, he comes stampeding back with a large shoebox. Beaming.

"Okay, I give up. What do we have inside our Nike box? Some bad-ass shoelaces?"

"Oh, man, this you won't believe. I'll blow her mind!"

He pulls open the cardboard top, reaches down inside, and...and... omigod...shrunken fucking *HEADS*? This is it, *this* is the mind-blower?

"From the jungles of Ecuador, man."

He announces this as both claws reach into the shoebox. "These are the real deal, man. Ecuadorian boiled and dried cannibal heads... A pal of mine, his uncle, in the jungles for five months. Alla these big boiling pots and fuckin' psycho crazy fuckin' cannibals, man."

I stood up and peered down into the Nike shoebox; there appeared to be four more of these things, whatever they were. Dour smirks on their tiny little dead, desiccated mugs. One had the proverbial bone thing through the nose. Legit? Hardly (maybe?). I didn't really feel like stroking the taut skin or eyeballing the features any closer; the shoebox reeked like a halfway cocktail of dried puke and humid sweat. Some sharp teeth. But the one he's dangling from his left hand, this one looks like, honest, an African American Richard Gere! Ha ha ha. Gimme a friggin' break. "Jones, where the hell did you dig these up, fry pots in goddamn Borneo, my boiled ass! Richard Gere there looks like some ring-toss prize from a JCPenney parking lot arcade."

"Hey, man. But I had you goin' there, huh?"

"Not really."

"But check it out, we get Sally here, and you can have Mel—I saw the way you were tracking her in the car before the woof letdown— and we'll have, like the WILDEST party, let's call it the *SHRUNKEN HEAD BALL*."

"Henry, I think *your* head's the only one which is shrinking to try and fathom reality. Sal was pissed—she didn't dig the dog circus...and—"

"Yeah, but that was because the dog deal went bad, man. That wasn't my fault."

"Yeah, but nevertheless, she wasn't impressed. And when you started howling and doing your coyote-yipping calls on the way home, didn't you get it? I mean, it was like they both sprinted out of the Beemer when the wild ride ended. What makes you think you're gonna lure her—them—with these Target toss-off pigmy heads?"

"BECAUSE OF THIS!" He pressed on the forehead of black Richard Gere—was it a switch? I couldn't quite tell. Abruptly, the head started bobbing and the mouth started moving; the cumulative absurdity of the motion was just over the edge. A bright red tongue emerged in synch with the movements of the mouth opening and closing. Mouth open, mouth open tongue protrusion, tongue retraction, mouth opens wider (yawns?), tongue vanishes, mouth closes abruptly. The sequence cycles until the forehead is depressed again."

Hank beams widely; he's really cracking himself up, imitating the battery-driven head with his own mouth and jaw.

"Okay, I've had enough," I yammered through the stillborn chaos. I reached for my keys, but Jones had the jump.

"Hear me out, man. Here's the story. C'mon, remember when you were telling me all the things you wanted to do with Melanie, but you weren't sure that she'd have any part of it?" Maybe this was half-true, minus the melodrama that Hank merges with all such reminders and recollections.

"Yeah, so what?"

"So what?" He was stomping up and down, swinging the ghoulish Gere face by its cheapshit synthetic tufts of hair. "This is your chance, man. The Plan, you wanna hear the Plan, I'm the Man with the Plan... man." I sighed and sat down. I was exhausted and, well, what the heck was the plan anyway? "What would be, like, just the ultimate wild cave scene?"

"Huh? I don't follow."

"Mel for you, Sal for me, that's wild wild wild, but I'm talking even wilder, way way wilder, man. Where's the wildest child hide?"

"Under the sheets?"

"Ha ha ha ha...that's hot, but not half as hot as what I have in mind, are you ready? We *get them to do a Lezzie thing for us*, wouldya think man?

"I think you've totally cracked your nut, Jones. Wait, let me get this straight: you jive up some jackass gimmick to lure Sal and Melanie here. Then you whip out your battery-driven shrunken head, black-faced Richard Gere with the cyst on his lip? You press the switch, and the tongue and mouth starts doing its thing. This gets everyone so worked up, particularly the guests of honor, that all propriety flies out the kitchen window? Sal and pal start pulling at their clothes, thrown into a rage they can't reconcile or snap out of, uhm, am I getting this right?"

"And they're, like, *hypnotized*," beams Hank, "the tiny mouth and the tongue on the voodoo doll, it's just too powerful, they can't resist. They're like, helpless—'cause they, like, relate to the whole shrunken-head legacy. It's in their blood; they're wild, wild chicks from the sub-Saharan jungle from maybe generations ago; many transcended past lives. They don't really understand this, but they're slaves to this hellish calling, to their sexual DN-fucking-A, man! Naked on the floor, they're writhing on top of each other, they've morphed into sweaty Paleolithic creatures. Hands all over the place. Hair flying on the carpet. And they beg me to give them what they all of a sudden really, really want. I'm ready, 'cause I've known what this would be from the moment it all started. And...that's when I take Richard Gere here, and I shove it in between... Well, I press the button and black Gere starts the fuckin CAVEMAN MUNCH, man...can you see it? And we all start howling like a pack o'woofs unleashed!"

Hands on the top of his head, he *shrieks!*—and then suddenly bolts down the hall. I hear a door slam shut, sounds like the bathroom door, but can't be certain. I hear water—bathtub? sink?—'cause the pipes in the wall seemed to echo a cascade of mortified screams and *howls* emanating from the nether regions of wherever he's seeking refuge, of whatever space his twisted, frayed neuronal circuits have chosen to regroup and converge upon a more stable equilibrium point. But the chorus of animal angst expires as suddenly as it erupted and then all the groans and commotion decay unceremoniously into hollow quiet. I can hear the wind picking up and throwing some branches of the tree outside the kitchen against the front gate.

I wake up the next morning in my bed, diffuse rays of sun awash over the floor and walls, and I'm not entirely clear whether I'd been transported back to Kansas and alla this had been some discombobulated ~~dream~~ nightmare. I pull the covers over my face, burrow down to the bottom of the bed.

(Just like when I was five and caught the original *Invaders from Mars* [with Arthur Franz] and, based on quick calculations interpolating the size of the holes in the sand dunes [that I scrupulously measured on my TV screen] that opened up and swallowed unsuspecting dune-strolling townsfolk about to get alien lobotomies, I arrived at the fact that the upper bound for sand dune apertures was in real life five and a half feet. Checked the math several times, five and a half feet. The consequent action that this necessitated was then clear: scrunch down to the bottom of the bed and HOLD ON TIGHT! 'Cause if a hole opened up in the floor of my room, it couldn't possibly be large enough to take the whole bed [greater than 5.5 feet wide and long] with it! I slept like this for three weeks until my folks discovered my sleeptime safety net one night and then I had to go see a kid person's headshrink [speaking of...] on a regular basis... Only after I demonstrated that I could sleep like a "normal" person for several days was I issued a grace period from womb-reflex analysis. I evolved to the conclusion that I'd rather risk going down a five-foot pit than endure kid encounter therapy. But not long after this, although I was forbidden to watch the TV series *Chiller*, on the sly at a sleepover with friends, I caught *The Four Skulls of Jonathan Drake*—and then I couldn't sleep below the window above the head board.)

But now the phone rings. And rings and rings and rrrings, and after six or seven of these I relent and grab the receiver to my ear under the covers, down deep in my fortress under the blankets at the bottom of the bed. "Yeah, whaa?"

And then faster than you can say "black Richard Gere," there are two sweet, almost obsequious-sounding voices on the other end. It's Mel and Sal.

I cringe, awash with guilt and relentless recriminations for the nightmare previously described. I apologize for the futile dog hounding of the other day; I apologize for Hank Jones's less than a laugh riot cartoon caricature of life. I apologize for throwing Sal into the position of fending off Hank's canine objectifications; I apologize for the long ride out to the Valley and the (uhm) hair-raising escapades en route. I apologize for apologizing so profusely. I'm sweating, but the voices at the other end are giggling and gyrating now.

Huh?

"Oh, don't be so recriminating, so…Jewish."

"But…that's what I am!"

"Guess where we are? Where we've been all night."

"Whaa… Where the hell are you?"

Melanie grabs the phone. In the process, I can hear her say to Sal, "Make him guess what we're holding!"

"Okay, never mind where we are, take a wild guess what I've got in my hands!"

Gregg Turner

"No clue..."

"It's, uhmm, way smaller than it should be, it's not happy, and it—check this out—USED TO BE ALIVE! NOW IT'S DEAD!"

"Uhm, a stuffed wolf. You got a stuffed puppy, how cute...how commemorative of that afternoon."

More than a forever pause at the other end of the receiver. They're now both convulsive with glee. "You're not even close! You want another clue, one more clue?"

I wanted back to sleep suddenly, but one more clue, I knew, was coming. "Alright, then, one more."

Sally gets back on. "Okay, here's the final clue—*movie actor.*"

Mel shrieks into the mouthpiece, "*PICKLE!*" and the phone drops.

They both sound sloppy and reckless. They're laughing loudly and making strange animal noises and I can hear, how appalling, Jones doing his Mountain Man yowl in the background. There's ungodly commotion, and then I hear him shouting, "Hey girls, whaddaya say we get that lesbie thing going again?" and somewhere in the room someone says, "Only if we can watch The Black Forest of Babes one more time!"

Mel and Sal start shrieking, "YESS! Black Forest! Hair! Pink tongues! Hey, Hanky," they hiss, "DO THAT THAT DOG TRICK YOU SHOWED US LAST NIGHT! LET'S PLAY DOGS AGAIN!"

I can hear him scream back, "You mean Leader of the PACK?!"

"Yeah, Yeah, let's play Leader of the Pack again!"

Then a dial tone.

"The Black Forest of Babes?" I managed to remember, in a marginal snapshot of time, that he used to joke that "his chicks" referred to the fine coiffed strands of jet-black locks perched topside of his head as "The Forest." So I couldn't decide whether to run to the bathroom and purge or fall back asleep.

Still, I wished I could be as cool as Henry "Hank" Jones.

IT'S A MOUSSEAU!

MAY 2013

1. Sheena was in fact a punk rocker but also a close friend over the years. Said she thought I was lonely and brooding and needed some female attention. Me, I couldn't care less, enjoying the quiet and solitude of not being around ANYONE, this being close to one year after a particularly brutal cessation of a four-year relationship. They say that in Santa Fe, for every available single dude, there are a dozen available (single) women. I don't know if this is, in fact, the case, but what they don't tell you is that nine of these femme fatale prospects are gay and the other three are whack jobs that have emigrated from Mendocino and Sedona with larger-than-life issues, existential buffalo chips on their shoulders that they expect to vaporize once they make the sojourn to the high desert. But more commonly they just tote this psychic baggage with them, nothing erased or eradicated from the damage and emotional detritus they leave behind. Or they set up shop and, once in town, become contaminated with everyone else's neurotic impulses.

So Sheena wants to set me up with her friend Gloria. Gloria is an audiologist now practicing downtown, been here only in New Mexico briefly and—so I'm told—Gloria has fled from a bad marriage of six years herself. Only makes sense for you two to commiserate, Sheena suggests, why not cross paths and share open wounds.

Now Sheena, it turns out, was a pal of one of the more suspect creatures in this city. Her name is Anastasia—Stazi, they call her. She boogies around the town towing a shopping cart of (her) clothes, these gypsy rags and scarves and so forth, and you can sometimes see her holding court saddled with her cart on the sidewalk below The Conejo Café (overrated rich folks' eatery). She is not a homeless soul, word has it, just a colorful vagabond. And late Friday afternoon, Stazi traipses around to the art gallery openings on trendy Arroyo Road. She walks into the Morrison-DuBrow Gallery, one of the higher-end art dumps on the street, drinks half a glass of Chardonnay, and munches on some cheddar cheese cubes and quinoa crackers. Then she goes to the gallery host and wants to know more about the papier-mâché donkey propped up in the window. The donkey is draped over with netting and an assortment of colorful towels. Big donkey. Maybe five feet high and six feet long. Cheesy piece o' crap that only this full-of-itself artiste emporium could have the temerity to ask $12,000.

Stazi asks about the artist. She's decked out more than disarrayed; her piecemeal scraps of motley rags fastened to her buttoned-down pink silk shirt parade an absurdity of fashion that's a welcome distraction in this pretentious gallery palace of pop-art dreck. The host ignores her query but faces a tourist couple who are requesting similar info and background. "Oh, this is the latest work of Gerard Goddard, the renowned sculptor and impressionist from the Laucerne Valley.

The couple gasp, "Oh, we didn't realize that this was a Goddard! Incredible!" Yeah, just fuggin' incroyable. But Stazi has already whipped out her checkbook. She pulls one out and writes at warp speed, "Morrison-DuBrow Gallery, $12,000 and no/100!" The host, Eduardo, grabs it, sighs, and shreds it to pieces in his hand. He asks her to leave.

Gregg Turner

She eventually makes tracks out of the gallery, then saunters into the Feingold Pantry of Fine Art. On the back wall of the front room is a painting of a woman holding a bouquet of flowers. Big-assed painting. Could be like four by six feet. A bumblebee is hovering above one of the flowers. The woman in the painting has a dour expression transfixed on a pasty face—the colors are drab and the depiction is lifeless and stiff. Still, Stazi digs it the most. And she asks the gallery host, Lars, for background.

"Look," he brushes her off, "didn't we have a conversation about this?" His petulance and dismissiveness is only surpassed by his impatience.

But she persists: "I enjoy the muted colors and how disaffected this woman in the painting is. She is unhappy with her life and emotionally constipated with how she is unable to express this."

Lars shoots back an annoyed twitch erupting from the corner of his right eye, radiating down the side of his face. They've been through this before. Last week. And two weeks before that. And now Lars is scouting the man in a cowboy hat and his trophy wife that have ambled from the street through the front door. Turning his back on Stazi, Lars runs over to the them, they are from Dallas they tell him. Lars licks his chops. He points to the row of paintings they are scrutinizing. "These are all by Henri Mousseau," he drawls, "an incredibly talented surrealist from Lyon."

"*Sweetie,*" the woman gurgles to her husband, "it's a Mousseau!"

Lars's eyes have a wide-on and he spits back, "This one is called 'Night Birds.'" And sure enough, there are birds, dark, spirited birds circling a pallid navy-blue-like lake, consumed by terse fog and nightscape-ish sky. Lots of birds—big birds, little birds, even a couple fat birds. But no hummingbirds. "Mousseau was a very private man, his sketches so passive, yet striking, with sharp paintbrush accents," drools Lars. He points out that the colors employed are "muted but with strident strokes." Stazi's heard enough—her hand quickly produces yet another check—this one payable to the Feingold Pantry of Fine Art for $7,500.00. "Sweetie" and his wife bugeye when they witness this little kabuki dance. Lars tears up the check, escorts Stazi out to the sidewalk, and, back inside, assures the couple that "Night Birds" is still available for purchase.

A block down on the other side of the road is the Morgenstern Gallery. Stazi trots down to the front door. Oh, boy, oh, boy, she really loves this place. She parks her clothes cart by a cottonwood tree adjacent to the adobe entry. Folks are noshing on wheat wafers and sipping from tiny beakers of white wine. This time she spots an original Dalí mounted with prominence on the featured gallery wall. But before she can unleash the checkbook, two suited gents lead her out the side door to the pavement and admonish her not to return.

So she hoofs it down Arroyo Road, tosses her cloth ornaments on a bench, and parks her cart. Two weeks later she disappears from sight. No sign or apparition of her countenance. Gone. Taken off. Splitsville.

2. Sheena tells me that Gloria will be shopping at Trader Joe's tonight and would like to hook up, maybe get something to eat. "She wants to rendezvous in the TJ's parking lot at seven; why don't you take her out to La Choza [primo red/green chile New Mexican joint]?" I reluctantly agree, don't know about this Gloria person, but La Choza is always pretty good and my stomach was making some serious empty-hole sounds.

We cross paths under the awning at the front of Traders. She is reasonably pretty, big eyes. Always a plus for me, though that was a trapdoor I fell through with Linda way back when. She's decked out in a fringe denim coat, dark blue trousers, and sandals. Seems friendly enough, nice smile. Maybe this would be okay. Get into my

Gregg Turner

car, her blue Jaguar is parked a couple spaces over. And we nudge out of the parking lot en route to the restaurant.

The place as always is packed, thirty-five minutes for a table. So we sit down on one of the couches in the waiting area. She asks why I suggested this particular eatery, and I offer that it's the best in town for New Mexican cuisine (she's a recent transplant from South Bend, Indiana—been in Santa Fe only a few months). Then she scrunches up her eyebrows and asks if the place is really worth the trouble. Maybe we should have just gone to Whole Foods and got something from the salad bar. I allow that we could scram and still do that, but she looks at me and quips, "No, you wanted to come here, let's stick it out. There must be some reason why you felt the wait would be worth it."

Uh, okay. So we wait. And wait. And keep waiting. Almost forty-five minutes have gone by now. Finally we're escorted to a table next to the fireplace. Sit down, look over menus, she asks what is good. Anything with red chile on it, I allow. Their red chile here is the best. She orders enchiladas smothered with red. I decide to go for the fish tacos with green salsa. She eventually takes the fringed denim coat off, places it on the back of her chair. Wipes her forehead, sorta hot, she notes, here by the fireplace. Was this the best spot to be seated, she asks? We could relocate, I tell her. "No. this'll be okay. But it *is* quite warm." She looks up at me: "You must be chilly tonight."

The food finally arrives, and she is scrutinizing the red chile sauce on her enchiladas. She tastes, recoils a bit, remarks that it's "pretty spicy." But "there's probably a reason why you would believe I like really spicy food. Maybe my red hair. Ha!" Yeah, that's it, I always presume redheads love that spicy food. She takes another bite, grimaces, puts her fork down, and asks why I chose to recommend "something this hot." Also, "Why didn't *you* get the red chile? You got green." I suggest we could switch, but she doesn't like fish tacos, she says. And by the way, it's super hot here by the fireplace (it really wasn't). Maybe we could move to the vacant table by the window. So we do this. However, the table by the window isn't steady, it's wobbling a bit back and forth—she observes "that's probably why no one's sitting here." Maybe.

She doesn't like Mexican (new or otherwise!) food at all, not a bit, she concedes. So after she scrapes off all the red chile from the plate, she decides she ain't into the enchiladas, and comments, "I guess you assume everyone in town, or moving into town, enjoys this type of food—I guess that's fair enough. 'Cause this *is* Santa Fe." Yes, it is, I admit. I propose we could still split to Whole Foods—it's open another hour. "Well," she duly notes, "then I suppose it would only be fair if you foot the bill here—I mean, you never really asked me if I like 'Chicano' cuisine." No *problemo*.

We tool off in my Subi to Whole Foods; it's only a few blocks away. But she's looking a tad uncomfy; *now* what's the problem? "Oh, it's okay. I think that red chile just upset the lining of my stomach a bit." Hmm. "But," she charitably adds, "you had no way of knowing this would be the case." Right. No way of knowing that consuming one half of a teaspoon of the stuff would trigger her IBS.

We slip into the WF lot, dash inside, and make it to the salad bar. She's looking around...around... "They have no marinated artichoke hearts," she points out, disappointed. "Back home, our Whole Foods always has these." She looks at me—"I suppose you don't eat a lot of artichoke hearts, or even realize that they don't have cooked beets here, 'cause we coulda otherwise gone to the Souper Salad place that Sheena was talking about." Yes, maybe that would have been a better option.

We sit down, catch a Whole Foods table in the back (no fireplace), spread out the salads, it's pretty crowded. Behind me. Weirdness. Someone growling. Muttering and snarling. Like a servile wolverine.

Why, it's LARS(!) and his boyfriend from the Feingold Pantry of Fine Art! "I thought those prissy Texas nitwits were gonna buy the goddamn Mousseau," he drawls. "But that raggy vagabond with alla the scarves on her, she's a real nuisance. Scared 'em away."

"That Mosseau is a nice piece," offers the boyfriend, to which Lars sneers, "It's a piece o'crap. The artist's name ain't even Mousseau, it's, like, Frank Berger, from Bakersfield, California, ha, but those stupid fucking Texans don't know shit, so you gotta call it a Mousseau or Saint-Pierre or some such BS." He frowns, contemplating the gravity of this. "And that goddamn scarf lady—man, I hear last night her name ain't Stazi, it's *Marlena Anastasia Rockefeller!*" He eyes the boyfriend, adds, "She's 'parently worth every fuckin' penny of the checks she was handin' out!" Looks down at the floor—"Can't find her nowhere in town, no sign or trace of that nutbone."

The boyfriend, Jean-Paul, looks at Lars and shakes his head. "Isn't that always the case, though?"

Not to be too conspicuous, I'd been looking down at the floor myself to catch the grift from these art drifters, and when I look over at my date (is that what she's been?), she's gone, absent, history! What the heck? Only a fraction of her food on the plate missing, maybe the red chile still acting up? Maybe she's on the prowl for beets and artichokes in the produce section. Oh, lookit—there's a note. How sweet. It reads:

"I don't think you were enjoying my company all that much. Better that I sneak off and say goodbye. I'll get an Uber back to Trader Joe's. Just a word of advice though...GET A PROFESSIONAL HAIRCUT!"

I thought about this. Why? I go to Great Clips every month.

SOME KFC AND GAS
MARCH 1995

"That'll be five dollars and eighteen cents," she said to the old guy who was on pump number five.

"Here," he fumbled in his pocket for the change and came out with a couple of coins, handed over a five spot and two dimes. She reached to the register to produce the two-penny change, but he said, "You keep it, darlin'." So she kept it and he smiled like he'd done his good deed for the year and ambled outta the gas and GIANT junk food one-stop.

"I'm on number fer," yapped the next gent in line, handing over his plastic. "I'm gonna do ten."

"Dollars or gallons?" she called back to him, but he was already out the door and the fat dude who was next threw down five big bags of cheese puffs.

"How much you pump?" she asked him.

And he said, "I didn't pump nothin', just the cheese chews." He sounded a tad pissed, like he'd been asked the same thing at the other gas stops—like, maybe one of these times it'd be *Okay* for a guy to just come in and buy dinner and not hafta feel bad fer not pumpin'. In a huff he turned around and took off—"fuckin' place," he said to no one in particular as his gut shoved the station's doors ajar. "Fuckin' world," he exhaled out loud outside where nobody could hear. He tore open the cheese bag with his teeth, reached inside to grab some in his extended sweaty talon, but the bag exploded from the force of his forearm—he was elbow-deep and it split in several sections. Still, he grabbed as much as he could and shoved it all quickly down into his mouth and bounded off across the street.

She, behind the counter, was about thirty-five-ish, big overbite with a capped front tooth and yellowing cuspids. Pretty tall and sorta skinny, lousy skin. Could tell she'd been working here for quite a while, had the motions to the register down pat. Didn't look no one in the eyes for more than a split second or two at the most. And you could tell that was the seasoned mark of someone really good at what they do—for this sort of thing. Did she have a name? You bet, and a real good one: "Lavinia." Her tag said "Lavinia," but here at the GIANT Superstop she answers to "honey" or "darlin'." Well, to be straight, some travel-weary creep walked in when it wasn't all that crowded, and he said, "Okay to fill it myself, ma'am?"

"*Ma'am*"! She 'parently liked that a whole heckuva lot, 'cause she shot back, "Why, sure is," surrendering a three-fourths exposed-cap smile. He tipped his hat, and went out to do his business.

Then finally no one in line, so Lavinia sets down and swigs a big gulp of unsweetened Lipton Iced Tea. Two swigs, but then a couple suits walk in, check out the freezer—no, they decide they don't want no ice cream. They go by the crackers and cookies, look 'em over— no, they don't want none of that neither. Lavinia tracks 'em outta the corners of both eyes. Maybe if she pretends she don't notice that anyone's there, they'll hang for an extra minute or so—an' she can stay stationed. Been on her feet all mornin', the extra seconds on the stool and the cold tea feel pretty damn good, she's thinkin'. One of 'em picks up an *Albuquerque Journal*. Starts readin' out loud to his buddy. "Goddamn hantavirus is gonna wipe us all out… Hey, Frank, they say that when those fuckin' deer mice meet winter, they're going to take for people's homes and stuff. And then shit's gonna hit the fan."

Gregg Turner

"Not if you don't breathe the rat piss," says Frank.

"But how do you know if you're breathing the piss or not? It'd be, like, invisible, right?"

Frank thought about this for a moment, then offered that if *he* lived around these parts, hell, he'd get himself a small army of cats—the cats would of course stay outside 'cause he don't like cats—but they'd "wipe out the goddamn vermin" since he wouldn't feed 'em or nothin', so the only way the cats could survive would be to off alla the mice.

"Yeah, right, then what happens when one of the kits parades around with a headless fuckin' rodent—into the house, or on the doorstep even? What then, bro?"

"Can you get the hanta thing from 'vaporated *blood* and stuff?"

"Well, they say just piss and shit, but isn't piss part of blood, bro? I mean, like, it's in the blood before it becomes piss. And what about the damn cats? If they're suckin' on the rats' eyeballs or pullin' out tongues and shit, you tellin' me they can't carry the thing themselves?"

"Well, no one ever said anything about cat piss or nothin'. 'Cause if that could make you sick too, they'd have said something already."

"Maybe not because the cat idea's pretty new. Ever seen a cat tear into a mouse, Frank? I had a buddy—he had two pet cats, one was called Justice an' the other, I forget what it was called, Tequila or somethin like that…but anyway, the Siamese, Justice, somehow gets a hold of this real fat roof-rat, or maybe a tree-rat or whatever, but he twists off its goddamn head, then pulls its feet off, and goes and dumps the stinking, bloody rat body, what's left of it, into the john and drops it smack down on the goddamn toilet seat. He says his wife was the one who found out, 'cause she hadda go real bad, y'know, and she sits down with her dress up—y'know not very ladylike how she throws it up in a hurry frantic to pee and all. And then in about two-tenths of a second she starts fucking wailing, bro. And I think it musta been there, the stinking stiff rat, for a while—'cause there were like shitloads of ants and crap—man, that musta been hell turned upside down!"

Frank thought about this for a bit, and then admitted resolutely, "Y'just can't let 'em in the goddamn house. That kinda shit happens... Cats gotta stay outside."

Frank and his bud finally take off, two Snapples and a Tuna sandwich later. "Quiet again, but not for long," she broods behind the counter. Some days feel like a coupla weeks—not the first time this thought's hit her dead-on in an existential-like way. But summer school at the college doesn't start for a while, so might as well enjoy the boredom. And just when boredom's starting to feel real good, in walks some sleazeball with super greasy black hair and a grimy, stringy beard. He's in torn jeans and a month-old tee, near forty-something—but it was hard to tell. He reeked like a mold-encrusted piece of rotten garlic bread and kept coughing and hacking up hard phlegm from the back of his throat.

"You pumpin' gas, Mister?" Maybe he'd get the idea his vapors weren't appreciated.

But he shot back, "Huhhh, wass thatcha say, honey?"

And she double-shot back, "I said, you want any...gas?" She was beginning to get really sick—both of the windows were wide open, but it was like inhaling the stench of Hades. Even dogs rolling in day-old hoss manure don't smell this fucking bad.

His eyes opened wide; she was talking to him. That was good, he thought. He liked her a whole bunch, that's what he was thinking, and found himself more than sorta excited at the prospect. "Well, honey, you're askin' if I got gas—I got lots of it!" He clamped his right hand on his rear, to perhaps demonstrate this reality, then offered, "Better not strike no matches, *heh, heh, heh*."

She imagined herself about three seconds from a serious hardcore heave, but then Lotty walked in with the chicken—coupla boxes of Kentucky Fried and some cokes. She trots past the stinky fuck and drops the boxes and the bag of drinks on the counter behind the register. "We were a few dollars over," she says, and she unravels some change to bear witness to this fact.

"Hey—these gals like that Froggy Fried Chicken!"

Lav and Lot look up, as in "huh?"

"That Froggy Fried smells reeeeel dern good. You gals must really go wild for that fried bird flesh, I betcha!" He stepped closer to the counter to get a better look. "Boy, I useta scarf bird all day long. In fact," he opened his eyes wide in this unreal sorta way and added "I STILL *DO* SOMETIMES!" And he started laughing and hollering. He clutched his stummy over his belt buckle—some kinda rodeo horse jumping a fence—and turned crimson red, convulsive with saliva and laughter. "These pretty young thangs jest cain't turn down that Froggy Fried Chicken! *Heh, heh, heh, heh, eh, heh, eh...*" And then he scooted out the doors and staggered off into the nether regions of the asphalt way past the pumps and finally out into the fields, and Lavinia looked at Lot and they stared at the cooler with all its cold drinks. They exchanged a silent vigil, but just for a few seconds, then reflexively pulled open the box of takeout. The slaw sure looked good.

THE SHEEP EATERS
JUNE 1985

"Seafood Salad, Seafood Salad
You can eat it, that is valid..."

The following is a fictional account of a fictional band with fictional people with no congruence to reality

Jeff Thornton was driving over the canyon with his rock band cohort, Morris "Moe" Edwards, guitarist of the big beat combo known as the Sheep Eaters. Click, KABC radio tunes in and the Sunday afternoon restaurant crit, Elton Kirk, was going on about his favorite gourmet dining experiences in the greater LA basin. As per talk radio, callers chimed in with their top picks as well.

This day, young Moe, six-string player extraordinaire and probably the most accomplished player in the band, was unusually buoyant. An angry, malefic dark side commonly hovered over the musician's psyche, and too often providence pushed the wrong buttons, unleashing a cesspool of incensed steam brewing like a veritable geyser behind both eyes. The bassist of the Sheepsters, Lou Ford, would normally play Moe for a fool, making fun of the fact that Moe wasn't the most swinging monkey in the tree (eventually Edwards threw in the towel and evicted himself from the lineup—no one could take the Frankenstein eruptions of rage any more).

Behind the scenes, while Ford routinely joked to everyone what a numbskull he thought Moe to be, he'd brag to Thornton how easy it was to manipulate the dude's anger internally (self-loathing) and externally (as a misanthropic miscreant) to suit his plans for the Eaters. Ford would routinely egg on Edwards, telling him that he, Morris, had been dissed outside of practice, presumably by Thornton and drummer Timothy 2-Sticks. Ford would not let up, anything to pull Moe's chain. He'd offer to Edwards that, out of earshot, Thornton had put down and mocked the masterpieces that Moe had scribed for the band; this would predictably drive Morris into a rage. Edwards' vokes and otherwise championing of "They Hacked the Devil's Crack" ("The Devil's Crack it kills at dawn, you need to find out which side you are on") was the right shot in the arm for lyricist Thornton, who badly needed to believe that something that low-grade ossified could be, uh, viable (and to be equally fair, it was Edwards along with Jett Call, the Eaters' interim bassist who replaced Ford when Ford split the band in the early eighties for a couple years—'twas Call and Edwards who put together the winning/rancid Iron Butterfly-inspired guitar hook that launched the tune. So Edwards had his shining moments. Certainly the inspirational Ramones-flavored opus, "(I'm Going) Down the Drain," was a permanent fixture of the live set, and let's not forget to mention the dude's role in "The Sad Story of Nathan Weiss."

Thornton and Edwards, frequently pals in various intervals of time, were thoroughly enjoying one of the few incarnations of Jim Jones biopics on the Thornton family TV in the den. This was the one with Powers Boothe (the John Agar of his day, truly a giant who towers above thespian colleagues) as Jones. "Drink the Kool-Aid, drink all the Kool-Aid, do not be afraid of the Kool-Aid, drink it all up..." Edwards and Thornton were rolling on the ground at this juncture in the film, nothing like a good mass-cult suicide to season an otherwise dull, dull day with rollicking waves of ghoulish yuks. Suddenly, responding to the chorus of glee from watchers of the Kool-Aid massacre, Thornton's aunt, in the next room, intoned, "Why must you be so entertained by the misfortune of others, of those poor, unfortunate Kool-Aid drinkers? Why can't you be productive and appreciate good things like your little brother's good friend, Nathan Weiss?"

This, of course, provoked more uproarious laughter from the Jones-cult watchers. Finally, Thornton walks over to Aunt Maggie and inquires, "What is it exactly that you admire so much about Nathan Weiss?"

Aunt Maggie thinks for a second and comes back with, "Well, he's nice and he's sensitive and he spends a lot of time in Florida" (in fact, Weiss was a House intern in DC). Jeff Thornton then scrupulously transcribes Auntie M's accolades (which continue for some time). It was only a matter of matching the suitable Sheep Eaters' response: "drinks booger water, eats pinworm-infested soy burgers, sucks rotten prune pits, chews candied genital warts," and so forth. Poor Nathan Weiss. With all of this, Moe was uncontrollably convulsive, serotonin molecules gang-jumping the primal receptors in his brain; this was, in fact, how "the Sad Story of Nathan Weiss" was conceived. But it would not have amounted to much more than third-grade grade school preadolescent-humor hijinks had it not been for Moe's inspired lead vocal. Don't downplay Edwards' charge here as merely a Thornton muse in the creation of potty music. Edwards' one-vocal take in the studio (no double takes necessary for Moe!) stands out heads and tails as perhaps penultimate road rage for the ages in the pantheon of punk-rock vitriol (reprised in the album's thirty-second seething outburst of torn psyche "You Filthy Creep").

For one thing, the ensuing recording session was hastily thrown together by George Entler, the producer for cult legend "Rocky and the Raccoons" back in the late seventies (at a later date, Entler begged out of Eaters' production credit, embarrassed by the foul fountain of vermin spew the record laid to waste). To begin, Entler enlisted, if you can believe, ex-Credibility Cleanlake bassist Lou Bakes, to use Bakes's studio. Nothing wrong with that, nice of Bakes to be so generous. Then comes time for Edward's voke on "Nathan Weiss."

Well, it wasn't at first obvious, past the explosions of vocal spazdom in each chorus and the Bing Crosby croons of verse, what would transpire at the end. Up to that instant in time—we all were mesmerized in awed reverence ingesting the waves of young Morris's vocal nihilism—no one would dare offer that this vocal performance should be excluded from the punk RnR Hall of Fame. Then much too suddenly, the take ends, and there's a "CRRR-ASHH." Now everyone's asking what happened to Edwards in the recording booth (the "Sad Tale" tails out in self-immolated croaking and misery).

"Oh, here he is," yelps Entler, who ran over to the booth to see what was going on. "He" was lying in a swell, inebriated, hapless pile on the floor (well below the recording booth's view window), the studio microphone apparently ingested and it took a couple yanks to formally retrieve the thing from the singer's S-ophagus. So when you listen to this track on the *Return to Tehran* CD, realize that what you hear, from the one and only one vocal take, is what the band got! The apparition of angsty Moe's gestalt-from-the-dead performance here so freaked out Bakes and his kid (in tow with dad conceivably to witness a live punk-rock recording experience), they became gonesville before you could scream "sucks horsey dick" (err, I mean "licks pony barf" and "eats elephant squirt"—other loser bands wallow in "horsey dicks," but not the Sheeps).

Edgy Lou Ford abandoned the group in the early eighties for nearly two years. In this envelope of time the band had already put together a portion of *Return to Tehran* and taped several cable TV episodes of *New Wave Scenesters* with singer Jett Call. More than not, the songs that, at this point in time, captured the attention of punkophiles and Sheep Eaters' fans, and served to catapult the album to some sorta hardcore infamy, were "Devil's Crack," "Nathan Weiss," and "Blind Man's Blues"—and arguably even "You Filthy Creep." Note that young Morris Edwards raged the lead voke on all four tracks.

Edwards was also a very funny guy. His thankful comic relief often entertained band members at much-needed junctions of stress and calamity. There was the time he, lead axe swinger R. K. Hooligan, and Tim 2-Sticks were fast asleep in their shared motel room at the fabulous Broadway Manor (roach trap) motel in the roach trap district of San Francisco. Seems they forgot to lock the room's door (leaving it ajar and open to the world) at the end of the night, all having passed out in sublime alcoholic euphoria. Beckoned by the collective braindead wavelength radiating out of that motel room, some lucky street indigent-fellow casually walks in and removes their wallets and pants, drenching the rest of their clothes with generous streams of fragrant vagrant urine. Lots of confusion and self-recriminations the next morning—but everyone had a good laugh, whatta bunch o' happy-go-lucky goofy kids this Edwards, 2-Sticks, and Hooligan combo turned out to be! Ho, ho, ho!

Still even more riotous was the time Edwards rented a room in a two story "mini" mansion with Thornton and Thornton's best friend Lee Gossler. The mansion, only several blocks away from the Universal Studios film lots, had a rich legacy of location backdrops for many cheesy Dracula installments and C-horror movies. But a brand-new horror show was about to rear its head on Cliffside Street.

Fleas, millions and billions of fleas, infested the backyard (which was extensive). Fleas in the ivy, fleas in and on the grass, fleas in the bushes, fleas just friggin' everywhere. Big fleas, little fleas, so many fleas a hundred thousand flea collars wouldn't make a dent. Gossler voted for calling an exterminator, and when one eventually arrived, the dude abruptly turned off his spray gun, assessed the problem as "industrial," and turned the job down.

Now, young Edwards didn't stand for no tomfoolery when it came to limiting the space he could roam. Certainly not a bunch of punk fleas were gonna get in the way of his outdoor R and R. But it was more than that. Edwards was determined to let the critters know who was in control. He'd handle this himself. The plan? March out to the thickest thicket of fleadom, drop drawers, and take a liberal leak. This, he reasoned, would not only send the fleas packing, but it would also serve as a valuable signal of marked territory—clearly all living creatures understood the ramifications of such an act.

The door to the side of the kitchen, which opened up to the most vegetative, densest of flea forests, had been bolted shut for some time. Warning signs to guests were posted, admonishing grave bodily assault should the door be opened and this precipice to flea hell traversed. But Edwards had other ideas. One afternoon, he unlatched this portal to the mouth of heck, walked out into a patch of weeds, dropped trou, and enjoyed a hearty whiz. Just as quickly, shrieks of Shrek ensued, and the next thing palpable was Edwards crying and screaming to get back in, cupping at least one hand over his flea-riddled scrotum. He burst through the door, wailing in agony, and made quick tracks to the shower, where apparently he did not emerge for several hours. There was also some stuff about pants that would no longer fit around a flea-munched swollen groin section, but that's hearsay, I'm told.

　　　　　　　　　　　　　　　　　　　　　Gregg Turner

Well, Edwards wasn't the only one blessed with Lou Costello moves. Wasn't there the time, somewhere on the road some place down the Gulf Coast, where Tim 2-Sticks had his own shining slapstick moments? Yes, in fact there was! Keep in mind that the Eaters could never bring the act on tour for more than a few weeks. This was because they couldn't get along; well, let's spin it another way: they were at the core angry, nihilistic jerks—and at any given moment this southern nether region of Sulphur-imbued psychic soup boiled over. Often Thornton was the de facto peacekeeper, separating Edwards from Lou Ford. But there were lots of other instances when Thornton and Edwards got into it. So sharing rooms on the road became a tricky proposition. One of these times, Thornton shacked up with Sticks.

Sticks was feeling rundown and sick, sure of the fact he was running a high fever. A thermometer reading assured a 99.3 temperature, but that was enough to convince 2-Sticks that he was in dire straits. So he embarks on a new strategy—let's tab or graph the pattern of temperature readings every half hour and scope out the trend. But there's more: convinced he needed to sweat it out (99.3), he duct tapes each of the air vents coming into the Marriot hotel room. All except for the bathroom, where he apparently fashioned his own little sweat lodge. With the room's heat now routed entirely to the bathroom, blankets from the bed transferred into the bathtub, that was where Sticks chose to lodge that evening. In the tub with blankets and pillow, heat pouring in, door shut tight. The problem was that when the hotel cleaning crew arrived to routinely disinfect the abandoned suites the next morning, they found the dude passed out in the bathtub, nada but his sweat-stained undies to cover up the midsection of his fever-imbued, pallid torso. The maid let out a banshee war whoop that could be heard all the way to Bloomington, Indiana. Sizing up the wasted humanoid apparition for an OD'd junkie, this instantly created a shitstorm that had Thornton running for cover and disavowing association to hotel management. See? 2-Sticks could be a barrel of laughs as well!

Maybe not half as hilarious was Lou Ford's granny, so-called "Gramma Ford." Remember the time (I do) that he flew the elderly woman out to the West Coast for Easter (or maybe it was Chanukkah)? The Sheep Eaters had a gig at the dump du jour, the Garlic Clove in Gilroy, California. Lots of creepy crawlies out of their hole for this one; the joint was pretty packed.

Now lemme tell you this—Lou Ford, when he wasn't setting up the band's gear on stage, had this thing for bathrooms, in particular the urinals in bathrooms, where he could seemingly stand forever, long after the last drop of pee-pee had evacuated his body. Often he would be seen marking up the band name on the walls above the piss pots—well, hey, everyone's entitled to their own formula to conjure psychic bliss. But special guest appearance at this particular show was the matronly Grandma Ford, who was not, how to put it, entirely innocuous amongst the slimeball kids—she was decked out in a more than formal blue evening gown! At some point in the festivities, Lou sneaks off to the crapper, and Grandma is told to watch the merch table— bumper stickers, records, T-shirts, and so forth.

So she's stationed there for more than what seems a reasonable amount of time pinch-merching for her grandson (where'd he go?) when a particularly gnarly little skunk of a punk comes by to check out the goods for sale. He keeps looking up at Gramma Ford sitting down at the table ("what the fuuu..." is the frozen expression on his kisser). Finally, he drums up the courage to open his yap. "Where 's Moe and Lou, where's 2-Sticks?" he demands.

Grandma Ford stares him down and announces quite formally that her second-generation progeny is *très* occupied in the bathroom (been there a while). To this pronouncement, the mohawked, multiply face-pierced, troubled teen, looks up and asks, "Well who the hell are you?"

And without missing a beat, she replies sternly, "Why, I—I am Grandma Ford." It might as well have been a buggered bishop telling a disparaged disciple to get fucked up the heinie. I can't possibly begin to describe how wide the eyes opened in this unsuspecting little creep; his gasp of horror could be discerned all the way to San Fran-fucking-cisco's Hate (grrr) Street.

Oh, but really, Morris Edwards was the trippiest clown to be found among this bunch of bad-ass jokesters. Remember the night he decided to go shave his head? Yes. I think it had more to do with communing with his skinhead legion of fans (the skinhead look was more prevalent in hardcore days than in punk-rock circles of earlier years). Over a trash can in the garage, and utilizing someone's scissors, he implored Gossler to do him bald. Of course, employing scissors to skinhead someone is a losing strategy. The endpoint looked more a result of botched chemo, little ragged bleeding clumps of splotchy hair nodules adorning a smarmy blood-messed base of skin, than anything approaching a shining, no-hair crown.

What to do? Hmmm. What happens next is emblematic of that which separates the true savant from, say, you or me. Young Moe runs to the market and purchases the jumbo-sized, twenty-ounce (industrial graded) tube of Nair. That oughta melt off the tufts of scabby hair outcroppings, still clinging to his now-semi-mutilated, blotchy scalp, he reasons. So Edwards liberally shmears his skull with the entire goddang tube and that's when the hounds of hell bellow madly. The skin on his head swells up several fold and the hair clumps come off, but now he looks like an outtake from the old *Outer Limits* TV show—y'know, when they beamed the aliens down through some portal in a parallel dimension and their skulls were more than half the size of their extraterrestrial bods. But wait!—here's still another move of which mere mortal creatures could only dare to conceive. It suddenly occurs to Moe that his uncle's Thanksgiving celebration is just a few days away, ohmigod! And Uncle Jim (who essentially served, at the time, as Edwards's financial life support and most stern surrogate parental unit not to be messed with) gets very mad at stunts such as this, but no problem, just slip on a FOOTBALL HELMET or wrap enough towels around the distended and scalded scalp skin to make a TURBAN. Either way, no one will notice anything unusual! A sly one, that young Morris Edwards.

But now Thornton and Moe are still cruising over the canyon in Sherman Oaks. As the car heaves onward to the Valley, Thornton in a creamy haze revisits the very first apparitions of Sheep Eaters back in Thornton's folks' garage. Back then, with the model of the way-rockin' New York Piledrivers as a template to mix ferocious with stoopid, plus a handful of *really* stoopid songs leftover from recent days as the proto punk-rock combo known as GULP, the Eaters were shopping for a more, let's say, accessible identity. Now around the same time there was a washed-up Wildman rockabilly cat named Hoodoo Howard. In the early sixties he in reality had a brief radio-played tune called "Like So Gone, Man." However, in this incarnation, nearly two decades later, he set his sights on the punk-rock scene, and what a punk rocker he turned out to be! He'd wear his trademark leopard-skin coat and grab his belly-bloated paunch and go nuts—jumping up and down, spinning in a circle, singing tunes that Thornton and Ford fed him, particularly the more than wild "I've Got a Bone to Pick."

Ford's younger brother, young Fitzgerald Ford—who, for a moment, exacted the duties of lead guitar in the band's primacy—didn't like Howard. He didn't think the guy was funny or even terribly repulsive, either way a liability. Still, a consulting inspiration to the Sheeps, lead singer-songwriter of GULP, "Mr. Gulp," chimed in that Howard was the ticket. With that nod and Ford and Thornton's votes of confidence, the die was cast. And cast it was at the San Francisco airport, where Hoodoo tried checking thirty feet of chain length through United Airlines security (this was sixteen years pre-9/11!)—his brave attempt at punk-rock posture. Did I mention that this was the first live show the Sheeps were to perform? And they were opening for Rocky and the Raccoons too! So the stakes were high; everyone wanted to impress, bolt outta the starting gate.

But backstage before taking center stage, "secret weapon" Hoodoo Howard is now puking his guts out. Stage fright? Turns out, he mixed his cheese "encharitos" (his description) with too many glasses of red wine. But if this wasn't punk rock, well, what *would* be?

That question was quickly answered when Howard finally bounded to the stage, lyric sheets in his hand (insufficient amount of time to learn words). What the freakin' hell was that around his waist that he was swinging over his head? Hard to tell 'cause the thirty pounds of chain length over his face and around his pants made it hard to gather extra details. But then, suddenly it was more than clear...the dude was swinging, like a jacked-up rodeo cowboy, a huge DOUCHE BAG, ready for some lecherous lasso move or two. He accidentally knocked over the microphone with it and then, bending down to scrutinize the lyrics for "Bone to Pick," taped to the stage, he unintentionally plummeted into the crowd as the bag suddenly constricted about his neck! His face turned bright red, the engorged, distended douche bag now seemingly ready to burst, when (what looked like) milk erupted and squirted out (from it) on some chick in the front row. Oh, this just had to be punk rock.

Fitzgerald Ford didn't think so, but he still had long hair, so what did he know?

Now back in present tense, the daydream rapture of the Hoodoo Howard days hemorrhage to a close, Thornton reengages contact in the moment with young Morris Edwards. On the afternoon AM radio, foodie critic Kirk takes a phone call. "Hey Elton, I just came back from Baja and I was really impressed with the seafood there."

Elton pauses and offers, "Oh, my yes, some of the best seafood, certainly the freshest, can be found in any number of excellent chowder houses down the Baja coast."

The caller keeps on. "Well, in particular, ya gotta be excited about that seafood salad down there, y'know what I'm sayin?"

Kirk rejoins: "Well, caller, what type of seafood are we talking about here? Of course that area is renowned for its fresh seafood, but what kind of salad are you referring to?"

The caller wasn't through: "Uhm, I don't think you're getting what I'm alluding to there, Elton. Ya know, SEAFOOD SALAD. IN YOUR FACE, get it?"

Kirk, still oblivious to the wiseass caller (alluding crassly to anatomical appropriation of female genitalia) pushes the guy for more info. "Well, where exactly do they serve the salad you're referring to?"

Caller returns the serve: "Well, if you play your cards right, you can get down and chow on that babe's salad anywhere it's offered, *heh, heh...*" Quickly, the show goes to a commercial. But the damage is done—Edwards and Thornton are just spastic with riotous laughter. Maybe this was the greatest thing young Morris has ever heard on the public airwaves, maybe the greatest thing he's ever laid ears to period.

"Fucking Seafood Salad, man, whew! What a fucking idiot that radio show host is. *Ha, ha, ha, ha, ha...*" And in no time, he was at it.

The song's words just flowed like unfiltered African-bee honey from an organic hive.

> *Seafood Salad, Seafood Salad*
> *You can eat it, that is valid*
> *Sammy Scallop says it best: that seafood smell is on your head*
> *Seafood Salad, Seafood Salad*
> *You can eat it, that is valid*

Genius. Seriously.

SNOW CONE

DECEMBER 1994

"So, Kevin, any thoughts on attending the exam tomorrow—when it starts?"

Kevin Matison was a sorta-okay student, now enrolled in a junior-level math class I was teaching at the College of Albuquerque. Had him before in other courses in the math food chain that I taught at C of A—he'd never demonstrated ability that was, how should we say, prodigious, but he could digest the main ideas. More than I can say for the majority of the kids. Still, the biggest obstacle in K's path had to do with, let's say, commitment. He was a badass slacker: an infrequent homework-doer (math-lousy for learning) and his attendance was crummy and he was way too cocky for a not-that-much-above-average concept-getter. He usually passed the courses, but to achieve this result often required a waterfall of nudging and not infrequent coercion.

Likes to ski, does he, glide those slip'ry snowy slopes down the mountain and not much else could or would compete for his time. C of A was a small, private Christian Brothers (same as the ones who make the wine) college, no more than about fifteen in any one class. Keeping the joint populated was the key. There was no public option for the institution's longevity, so the paying customer—or, more to the point, the paying customer's folks—was the bread and butter of the college's existence. C of A probably was fifth on the list of academe hot-spots these kids wanted to attend, but just as probably the only place where they'd be accepted (i.e., institutions number one, two, three, and four weren't exactly banging down doors to recruit these kids). But ABQ and Santa Fe have serious-sized peaks behind town, and when the weather turns cold, and the cold can weather the turn of the season, then that must mean *snow*, which ushers in a whole 'nother set of attendance and concentration problems. They just disappear to the Sandía (means "watermelon") Mountain Crestway, and once in a while reappear in class when the alpine ice turns too alpine-icy and/or slick to prance upon. You take what you can get at this place: a few hip kids who actually are sufficiently adroit to capture the learning curve, or otherwise sparse but searching souls that sometimes surface.

Still, despite the fact that these emerging surface-days were the anomaly, you learn to seize opportunity. These infrequent instances amounted to once-in-a-while charged moments when they put aside their sloped-out snow orgies and emerged with ragtag texts and a handful of notes and questions that might make some sense. Most of the snow holidays took place in the posterior daze of the fall semester, so boo-hoo for these kids' chances of passing final exams. And low validation for instructors trying to believe otherwise that their teaching gig somehow smacked of, uh, significance.

Shelly was a big-eyed snow bunny who'd wiggle in and out of her chic REI costumes. The poles she clutched to navigate the turns down the hills were tethered tighter to her carcass than any aspiration of, uhm, intellectual epiphany. Generally speaking, the engine of logical circuitry upstairs in her head often professed atrophy and, as a result, unlike Kevin, Shelly could not begin to even occasionally compensate for her spattered attendance and overall vacuity. So subsequent snow sex overtures offered as exchange for passing marks came off hollow and disingenuous (less the thrill?). Besides, no student sleeper was I. That was a cave I never dared or cared to spelunk, not so much just for propriety sake, but very bad for the self-esteem and career implications. Hard to say in what capacity I excelled in the teaching biz, and what I was doing at this peculiar fifth-rate joint of lower learning.

Scavengers and confused grade wretches were the only semblances of life making office appointments that week. S'posedly Shelly was there to discuss why nothing in class had registered since the first couple of days. But quickly that passed to enthused anecdotes, hers, of the "body rushes, man" when the run down the hill is finished. Very frosty sketches, I was treated to, of after-hill sexing with alla her buds and bud-ettes even(!), because "we're just all so pumped up, man." Flattered, for a moment, that she confided to wax poetic in my direction of such after-slope escapades, more than satisfied to know that following the ski aerobics on the hill there was a continuity of athleticism.

"School sucks." She was looking down at the ridiculous Indian blanket on the floor of my office. "I have a hard time concentratin', man."

"Anything I can do," I asked, "to steer your focus back to books? I mean, do you read *at all*?"

"Oh, sometimes, I guess. I read *People* when I'm waitin' in doctor's offices and that kind of stuff, but the math really turns me off. It just isn't any FUN, man. It's fucked up 'cause I need this class for my pharmacy degree."

"Well," I mused, "can you imagine any way I might present the ideas so they are more *'fun'* for you?" No double entendre here, not even a single or half entendre. This was a serious matter and it required a sober facade to convince this kid I was serious, about her success, y'know? But she looked at me and doubted the credulity that I'd momentarily summoned.

She conjured a nasty grin, more than all of a sudden, and that's when she asks, "Hey!" her eyes beamed confidence and trumpeted alla the fun fun fun in the fun-filled universe I could ever imagine. She took the initiative—office door slammed shut and she snaked her fingers up along my knee, looked into my eyes with a gleam and a half and this ridiculous smile and blurted: "Hey, you ever had a *snow cone*, man?"

"A *what*?"

"Okay, I'll just say it," and then she just said it: "I'll give you a fuckin' snow cone for an A on the final, man."

➵●

Black ice, prevalent on the winding mountain roads up to the resorts at this time of year, was more than a nuisance. Frequent pileups were chronicled in the papers. Still, despite the encouragement to do so, not everyone trekked up and down the slick asphalt jungle of curves and ice flows with tire chains and vigilance.

"I may be a few minutes late for the exam tomorrow," Kevin offers. "There's, like, fresh powder and I'm slated fer doin' a few lessons." I could feel the steam brew behind my ears. Why the eff do I even bother? Sure enough, the next day, as advertised, he ambles in, way more than a couple dozen clock ticks late, so I'm radically PO'd. We get into it.

He stares me down, lodging his flanks on my desk, and, exasperated, maintains that there was "black ice" (but I thought he said "*black guys*") in the road, "all over the place. In fact, man, the cops stopped traffic to clear it all out."

"What? Black guys?" And he's hearing "*black ice.*" "What were they doin' up on the hill?"

"It's cold, man. Roads get icy. Damn black ice always shows up. All over the road."

"What? What're you talking about? Why were they all over the road?"

"Uhh, 'cause of the weather, duh? What do you think? You just gotta be careful, man."

"Careful? What're they gonna do? I still don't get it... What're you talking about?"

"Look, I'm sorry I'm late. I'm trying to explain that if wasn't for the all the black ice I'd have been here on time. So gimme a break, man."

"Well, just how many black guys were there?"

"Road was covered all over the place, more black ice than I'd ever seen before. The road was just swarming with..."

"You hit anyone?"

"I fuckin' drove over everything, until I skidded outta control off to the side of the highway."

"You call 911?"

"I toldja no one was hurt."

"But what about the black guys?"

"Still there, man, I guess. Still cold enough."

The class had long ago stopped writing, the chapter exam was crashing to a halt, and all concentration riveted to Who's on First.

Matison, clearly not sure why all the confusion, adds, "Eventually, the Highway Patrol cleared it all out, man. Just salted the road down, black ice all eventually melted, but..."

"They melted? What does that mean??"

Snow bunny in the front row runs up to the blackboard, grabs a piece of chalk, and writes in large letters: "*BLACK ICE* / BLACK GUYS."

She revels in her detective feat, the room cracks up, and boy, I feel even more ridiculous. Kevin looks up at me finally and yaps, "Too late to take the test, doc?"

This was the same group of kids I had the year before in an experimental semester workshop that was called "Counting Infinity." Lots of heavy puzzles and geek-enriching paradoxes offered to theoretically stimulate and/or enhance brain cognition (usually no takers).

"Sooo," I began my infinity spiel, "how do you know there's actually a square root of 2, for instance? Recall that the square root of 2 is a number, when squared, i.e. multiplied times itself, is equal to 2. For example, the square root of 9 is 3 since 3 squared, or 3 times itself, equals 9. The square root of 16 is 4. The square root of 10,000 is 100. But identifying an *exact* square root of 2 is trickier. Try the square root button on your calculator. Press the square root button and you get something like 1.414213562 but when you multiply this times itself (i.e., actually squaring), you get 1.999998. In fact, even the fastest supercomputer on the planet cannot produce a number that, when squared, yields *exactly* the number 2."

"Well, screw this shit," cried some dude in the back. "There must be some number, when squared, that comes to exactly 2. Okay, what about 11?"

"What about it?" I replied. "Eleven squared is 121."

"Then how about 1,000, man?"

"One thousand squared is a million."

"So what're we supposed to do?"

"What to do? Well, there's really nothing *to* do. It's all a matter of faith that there's a real number somewhere out there whose square is exactly equal to 2, even though we cannot numerically identify or name it. But instead of merely ascribing this to a measure of faith, per se, we just call it an *axiom*. If no such 'exact' square root of 2 existed, then there'd be a gap in the real number line, don't want that, so we create a fundamental assertion that no such gap exists. Pretty sly, eh?"

I continue the pitch: "See, although we cannot specifically ID such a beast (hafta produce an infinite string of decimal digits to do this, and that would take, uh, way too long), we accept that it's somewhere out there (a consequence of what's known as the Axiom of Completeness) and give it the name square root of 2.

Snow bunny didn't cotton to this at all, she being one of nine enrolled here for a liberal arts math credit, presumably pre-snow cone days, or before she set her sights on pharmacy school. "So what the phuck?" she offered out loud. Well, wtph indeed!? I was hoping for discourse; perhaps this would be the trigger to get things going. Better than the stony silence that haunted the first four or five presentations. Now, it seemed, they were letting me have it: "Like, who the hell cares?" She frowned, and then more resolutely crowed out, "You're no better than the fucking Christian Scientists, man. It all boils down to *God*, and who believes in what. I mean, are there *atheist* math guys, ones who *don't believe* in the square root of 2 or any other friggin' *acts-of-man*?"

"You mean *axioms*?"

"Yeah, acts-of-man, whatever," she retorted, more than a bit frazzled with all of this.

"Yeah," open traps another in the back row, "can you believe in the square root of 2, then, and not believe in *God* at the same time?" Well, this wasn't exactly the thought schema I had hoped to jumpstart, but maybe they were waking up. Maybe they were finally stretching their neuronal synapses and ready to be invoked, on one level or another.

"Well, who wants to count to infinity today?"

"I do," spirited a fresh kid in the front. "*I* want to count to infinity!"

"Okay, let's do it," I rejoined, like a psychotic cheerleader on mushrooms. "Everyone, repeat after me: 1, 2, 3, 4, 5, 6, 7 ,8...32, 33, 34," they chimed in.

They kept going and going. I couldn't break the cadence, put the brakes on *anything* till they hit "58." Maybe they woulda gone to 4,000 if left uninterrupted (one of the group confessed later on that she was "ready to count to a million, man, *if need be.*" Compliance was not the problem).

"Alrighty," I intoned over the fragmentary pronouncement of integers still randomly spewing out into the air. "Now let's count all the positive *fractions.* Are you ready?"

But before I could lead the cheer on this one, several jumped the gun and began shouting out things like, "4/5," "Pi," "Circle."

"Uhm, 'pi' is not a fraction," I corrected, "nor is our old buddy square root of 2. These facts turn out to be rather subtle and can actually be proven. You see, fractions are numbers that can be expressed as the ratio of two integers, like, say, 4/5, or even -26/3 or ½. Five can be written as 5/1, so it too can be expressed as a fraction, or in math-speak, a *rational* number. And just like the positive integers that you were all counting out loud so wonderfully a second ago, I claim we can count out all the fractions or rationals in a similar fashion! As a sequential, unending list."

"But before we get to this, let's start with counting all the positive *and* negative integers in the universe."

Before further prompting, they resumed counting out where they'd left off: "59, 60, 61, 62 and so on..."

"Wait, wait a minute...how about all our *negative* integer friends?! If you keep counting that way, we'll never get to *them.*"

Ski bunny starts counting, "-1, -2, -3, -4...how long you want me t'keep goin,' mister?"

"Well," I hastily offer, "I was thinking more along the lines of counting *both* negative and positive in the same list. Check this out," I offered: "Zero, then 1, -1, 2, -2, 3, -3, 4, -4, and so forth. You get the idea?"

"But what about 50?" someone says in the back.

"Well, that'll be there too, eventually. If I kept counting in this fashion I would've arrived soon enough at 50, see?"

Another one comes back with, "Well, then what about *150*, man?"

"Uhh, sure, that'd be part of the list too. The point is, no matter what integer you target, our ordering of these numbers will eventually include it, you see? That's precisely the point. We wish to construct a listing, an ordering, of all the positive and negative integers, not one excluded, in one complete list. The fact that every element in a particular set of numbers can then be counted in this way, listed in this fashion, allows the set to have a special property. We call such an infinite set, appropriately, '*countable*.'"

"Then how about *two* hundred and fifty?" the kid proposes once again.

"Uhm, yes, 250 will eventually be identified in the list as well."

"What about -6,000?"

"Uhh, well, yeah, that too, but you see…"

"What about a million?" darts a plaintive cry from the one who'd earlier confessed she was ready, on the spot, to count to a million.

"Okay, one million will be accounted for, it'll pop up eventually if we follow our list of numbers in the prescribed pattern that we adopted. Do you follow?"

"What about a fuckin' BILLION, man? Is that there too?"

"Yes, uhm, it will be there as well…if you keep at it long enough, they'll ALL be there, that's the point. All negative and positive integers, they'll all be there, that's what I'm getting at." A couple got up off their chairs and started to holler:

"8,910?"

"-2 trillion?"

"Uhm, how about 755, man? Will that one be there too, in our list?"

"Yeah, but you see…"

"Then how about 881?"

"Uhh, let's go over this again. Class, after me, '0, 1, -1, 2, -2, 3, -3, 4, -4, 5, -5, 6, -6…' You get the picture? If we proceed in this fashion, at some point, eventually, we'll 'get' to every positive and negative integer that exists. No positive or negative integer will be neglected. It's not a matter of how *long* it takes to reach various integers, but that reaching each and every one is feasible; it's inevitable as the list continues on."

"Hey," responds a brown-eyed girl, "so what about five BILLION TRILLION? Even if this is one we'll 'get to,' as you say, one that's gotta be in the list, I don't wanna be old enough to know how long it *took* to get there, you see what *I'm* sayin'?"

"Yeah," shouts another, "Shit, yeah. This semester's gonna be goddamn over before we even *reach* the fucker. So I don't get it, what's the point? Are you just tryin' to let us know that there are some numbers that are just like SOOOO big that we can *never* get to them, count to them, mention their names, even if we, like, live to be forty-three years old?"

"That's right, and what about 43, that part of your list too?" yipped out another one in the back.

One last attempt: "You see, it's not a matter of whether or not we actually *announce* the name of the number in our counting process. The gist is that every one of these numbers will eventually be *included* in our list, in the set. You get it? That's all that matters, that our list will include, by the very nature of how the pattern plays out, everything, all positive and negative integers, dig?"

"So you're saying that we don't actually have to *say* one million, it's okay to know that it'll be included, be represented in this list, at some point?"

"RIGHT!" (Light at the end of the dim tunnel?) "The pattern of how we proceed to list the numbers suggests that the inclusion of the number 1,000,000 is a done deal. Look, we have an infinite ordering here. The fact that we can order this infinity of critters in a sequential pattern is significant. This grade or quality of infinity is called *countable*. There are infinite sets—for example, the irrational numbers, numbers that *cannot* be expressed as fractions, like square root of 2 or pi and so forth—and this set of infinite creatures is understood to be UNcountable. An infinite uncountable set is so large there is no possible sequential listing or ordering of its elements. It just dwarfs the size of a countably infinite set. Think of all the stars in the sky; these would be countable. But the blackness surrounding all of the stars is uncountable space. The ratio of countable to uncountable is zero!"

"Hey, but I don't get what happens when we actually arrive at one million? If naming it isn't so important, then what do we say? Like, we can count 999,999 and then we don't have to actually say 1,000,000 next, and then keep going, say, like, *one million and one* next, like we're in denial, man?"

"Well, actually, -999,999 is the one right before a million, in our ordering, but..."

"3,400, will that be in the list?"

"How about -620, man?"

"AND WHAT ABOUT 43?"

THE TAPEWORM STORY

FEBRUARY 1979

Author's Note:

I have told the T-story many times. How many times? I've lost count—Fifty? Five hundred times—what difference does it make? Let me say this—I used to gnaw the raw flesh of fish at Sidewalk Sushi on Lincoln Street in Venice or at Sadie's Sashimi on Fairfax next to Cantor's. I'll be the first to confess: I wanted to be cool, to be popular, to be just like everyone else. In the beginning, I would order the teriyaki with rice, but, after a while, the hungry pressure of peers coerced indulgence. Initially I was hesitant ["c'mon, man," they chided, "swallow the sucker—this shit's too expensive to keep under your tongue like that"]. But then it wasn't long before I, too, was scarfing the stuff, sucking down those slimy slabs of scales like a manic penguin in a tide pool.

Now, I no longer continue this practice. Why? Because someone cared. Cared enough to clue me in to the repercussions of such squirrelly hedonism. The violation and degradation of the sanctuary of one's intestinal channel by a voracious, suppurating, forty-foot worm is... nightmarish and, most certainly, hideous. I was lucky—spared such a twisted fate. Not so fortunate was the poor ravaged rascal depicted in this account—who ultimately became a veritable worm hotel, all from a one-night sushi binge. For this reason, I feel obligated to recount the sordid details. I come to no conclusions and render no judgments about various lifestyle choices. Ultimately, you are the one who must conclude and choose.

It began like this: The wife found him standing in the bathroom, over the toilet, with one pant leg down to the knee (other one just above the ankle), and he was just moooaning ferociously. "Oh-whooaaahh, whoh, ahh, God, help me..." But she was not God, so she could not help. She was just the wife-person, now staring at, well, it looked like ten inches or so of some sort of WworrrrrmmmmmM creature protruding vigorously out of the husband's trembling, frightened hind end. And from the way this worm fellow was flapping and gyrating, banging to and fro against her beloved's butt cheeks, it did not appear overly thrilled to have emerged from what one might imagine as the dank, quiet sanctity and nurturing of a spongy, fully nutritious colon.

Full?? Well, this was the crux of the problem, of course—as cruxes go. It seems the guy had been radically constipated, 'kay? I mean, for quite a while (two months?). How do *I* know? Ask Jackie Mueller' she was the one who told *me*. In fact, her dad, an internist in Century City, has been doctoring the dude for a long time. *How* long? Geez, I dunno, you'd hafta ask her. But when I say "doctoring the guy," I don't mean for *worms*, per se. More like the usual stuff—a 'roid or two, nasal polyps, plantar warts—then a couple months passes and it's clear that this fellow hasn't had a regular bowel movement, *nada primo peristalsis*, for quite a period of time. So they eventually decide that this is not good and go through the usual battery of tests and so forth. But everything comes out negative and he's just not responding to any of the various medications prescribed. Which then prompts a ration of Metamucil and supposedly that doesn't do much either. On the other hand...

It's two weeks after Christmas, and all through the house no one is stirring—except for this poor louse, who's screaming his guts out 'cause some extra-massive slimy critter is slithering out of his arse, fourteen inches long (notice that an additional four inches have emerged since the previous paragraphs—this is not to be construed as overly eager hyperbole; in fact, the worm's rate of protrusion is about two inches per paragraph as we speak). And it's flapping about wildly, undulating and writhing, contorted in shape—dripping and slickly coated with, well, its host's intestinal juices from someplace inside—a warm worm lubricant nevertheless—creating a splashy, messy texture on the poor man's quivering flesh, easing its way out from a dark abyss. There was stench too. You just can't have fifteen inches of protruding tapeworm, slime-slated with digestive juices and related intestinal gunk, and not have stench. So there was that, to be sure. No doubt a sensory picnic for the wife as she happened in on this grim bit of performance art. And the worm? *Way pissed off.* Now he has major anger issues to deal with—much more at home playing the role of a well-kept parasite deep, deep within. Errr, just *how* deep are we talkin'?

An appalling thought, but it's all she can think of. Her pulse rate adequately amped, wife runs to the phone, legs scramble through the den to the kitchen. Lunges for the phone, calls the doctor. Answering service. Oh, my god, oh, my god (cascading groans of revulsion now suddenly more vibrant from the bathroom). Hangs up. Hospital? No, try service again, doctor's on call (worm-ridden hubby moans: "ohhh, dooo something—Helen!" [*the wife? is that her name?*]—"it's getting *bigger*—oh, shit, it's on my thigh, I think").

Helen finally reaches the doctor. It's 3:00 a.m.—or 4:00 a.m., something like this. He tells her that this is a serious matter, not to be taken lightly, must do something pronto. So then...

"*What? C'mon, Sarah, what're you making a face about?*"

"*Oh, sure...like the doctor's gonna say, 'Hey, don't sweat it, go back to sleep and in the morning if it's still a problem make an appointment'! Right! This whole thing didn't happen, gimme a break.*"

No, in fact, you're ahead of me—if you'll let me go on? Okay? Okay, so the exasperated doctor insists that they both meet him at his office without delay. Do not pass go or collect...whatever. Come straight to the office for worm extraction. And he'd arrange for some assistance, but the pressing matter was to de-worm ASAP. High priority to get the entire beast out before...

"Before what?"

Well, before it retracted back into its original living "space."

"Gross. So how could they be sure that wouldn't happen?"

Well, that's the point. They didn't *want* that to happen. I guess it's easier to remove the entire thing when there's some part to grab hold of and tug. I mean, otherwise...anyway, here's what the doctor told the wife: get some duct tape and try to tape down the flapping end to the butt. That way it can't *go* anywhere!

"No way! You're making this up! 'Cause that's really disgusting."

I am an investigative journalist. I do not "make things up."

"So you're tellin' us, what you're sayin' is, that there's this guy with some sort of heinous wriggling worm comin' outta him, out of his back end, like a house on fire—taped down to his butt so it won't go back inside; and he's headed for the doctor's office in the middle of the night to get it yanked?"

Pretty much.

"And you're saying that the doctor's there, with nurses and stuff waiting for this guy, and they're gonna yank the sucker out?"

Right. They needed to determine if it had subdivided or deposited any eggs or that type of thing. Whether it's one single worm, or, uhm, part of a worm *cult*. Maybe a whole cub scout troop of invading parasites..

"So then what happened?"

So, if you give me a chance, I'll tell you... They pulled it all out, they got it all.

"All what?"

Well, all twenty-six feet of it.

"No effin' way!"

It was like one giant worm thing. Had been living in the intestines for a period of time—I don't think they ascertained just how long, but for a while. Apparently intestinal waste and related dreck traveling through the digestive tract are steak and eggs to a hungry tapeworm.

"So what did they do, just reel it out like fishing line?"

And carefully, I suppose. Didn't want it to snap (or tear?).

"Did it?"

They put it in a pail—or whatever could double for a large enough specimen jar, and packed if off to a lab.

"Wait a minute, why did this happen in the first place? Why'd he have a worm? Did he like not ever wash his hands before...or after...?"

Well, I don't think it was a hygiene issue. Bad sushi, they're saying. Lots of parasites thrive in the (raw) flesh of fish. In most cases, the hydrochloric acid in your gut kills the buggers—but, evidently, not always.

So after it was pailed, they sent it off to the lab. I really don't know about these other things—remember I'm just relaying to you guys what Jackie told me. And—well, I wasn't there—in the office, y'know—when they were tugging the thing out.

"Well, so what about the worm-man. They got it outta him, took it away—and so now he's standing there, suddenly, with a clean bill of health? Did he wig? Was he relieved? Is that the end of the story?"

From what I understand, he was okay, everything was still intact—do tapeworms have teeth? But apparently the major problem at this stage was his *mental* health—or lack of it. He, uh, wasn't doing too well with, what did they say it was? *Letting go*, I think. For example, in the days that followed, there were these massive anxiety attacks. He would imagine a variety of *worms*, coming out of his eyeballs, worms suddenly erupting out of grape-like purplish blisters on the skin of his back and arms. Brain worms! He dreamed his skull was a planter box, his cerebral folds devoured by hundreds of thousands of tiny, pin-sized crawling things—and (in the dream) he lived the remaining balance of this worm-deformed existence with a hollow head. Just a worm-gnawed shell.

[*Sarah's friend Artov Leopod, a veterinarian from Budapest, has been patiently taking this all in, and now offers his two cents:*]

"*Ziz iz vot he had dream of? Zat vairms, zay ate his brains to nossing, and he leeved ze rezt of hiz life like a pazetic cockroach or zomezing zuch as ziz? But zay deedn't really do any of ziz, yes? Ven he voke up, he still had his brains? Zay vere ztill een hiz head?*"

There were a series of nightmares that repeated—and then the visual hangover of this apparently burrowed into his thoughts during the day. So for the first few weeks after the tapeworm had been extracted, he was more than mildly tormented, borderline dysfunctional. The wife, for instance, one morning—we're talkin' maybe a week post-worm—discovered him alongside the shower stall in the bathroom, taking his pants off—putting the pants back on. Taking 'em off, then putting 'em back on again. Off—on. Off/ on. Offfff... And so finally, with persuasion, he finds his way to a PTSD stress shrink. 'Cause at this point, he can't really work, won't eat, semi-catatonic—maybe too many cognitive worm-oid intrusions throughout the day (there was this one time, about a week after he'd been de-wormed, when he and the wife are driving home and they decide to cruise Dunkin' Donuts—she orders this raspberry jelly-filled thing, but he grabs it and starts pulling down his pants, and, well, I'm off on a tangent here...). Anyhow, they drag him over to a particularly well-respected psychiatrist, a Dr. R. O. Fiss, specializing in posttraumatic stress. The wife called to make the appointment.

Gregg Turner

"Hello, Doctor. This is Helen Beckman. I left a message on your service last week describing the problem... You got it?... Oh, great—okay. Well... No, the worm has been removed... Right. They got all of it... Yes, that's correct, thirty-eight feet... No, I don't believe there was any, as you say, degradation of, well, any part of the lower intestinal tract. No... Uh, no... the intense itching has subsided and the phantom food-worms are apparently gone also. That's right, he can even eat my spaghetti again... Well, okay, so the problem now is that even though he's free of worms—or worm—he can't let go of it. It hangs over him like a swollen, black rain cloud. He's morbid and dreams of small, antlike things, call them worms if you will, eating his brains out. He gets panic attacks during the day, and can't go to work... Right, no, that's right. He's been home for about a couple weeks now... No, as far as I've been able to tell, he has no unusual rituals or compulsions... No, well, I haven't seen him examining his—that place—since the other night... What's that?... No, I don't *think* he's done anything like that again or—tried to insert any *other* types of objects in there. Right. No, that's correct. In fact, I was behind the shower curtain watching and... I'm pretty sure he didn't see me... No—that wasn't the time with the Bactine, that was the time before... No, I agree. I think you're right, that'd be the best way to proceed at this point... Okay, so we'll see you next Thursday at two?... Okay, great... I'm sorry, what's that?... No, I will. I'll keep a close eye out and, I mean, I could watch behind the curtain again if you think... No, no, I don't keep any of those around the house anymore... Right, nothing that would fit in there... There *too*?... Well, okay, I guess that makes sense. It wouldn't hurt to be overly vigilant about this... Right... Right, I see what you're saying. Okay, thank you for the time, Doctor, and we'll see you on Thursday."

"*Now, vait vun zecond. I am trying to azzimilate ziz phone call you zhpeak of, but didn't you zay zomezing before about a, vhat vaz it, a pump?*"

A what?

"No, you know, a devize. An inztrument of zorts to eradicate ziz vermin, ziz horrible peztilence, forever. An enormous pump—vith tremendous zuction or hydraulic capability, ja?"

But they got all of it out, all forty-four feet of it. Why would they need additional equipment or, as you say, devices?

"But zats ze point, I am zaying. Ziz phone call indicates ziz man, ziz poor unfortunate vairm-infezted bug-trough of a man, to be haunted, no? Tortured vith ze zpectre of living out hiz life az a vizzeral vairm farm. A human hotel for zings zat infezt vun'z kishka—and zen protrude out and vriggle. Zo that perhaps a pump, I offer, might convince him zat ziz iz not nezezzarily ze case? Ziz doktor on ze phone, ja, maybe haz vun of zese types of pumps zere in ze office like ze ozzer doktor had ze bucket. So zay can pump him, for a long period of time if nezezzary, and vhen I zay pump him, I mean to zay—pump him good—zo zat zen he believes, or I should zay agzepts, zat hiz vairms are all gone."

Well, the salient point here is that none of this turns out to be necessary. They go see the psych—and the tact employed is one of *acceptance.* You know, I'm okay, you're okay, the worm's okay too! Heal your inner tapeworm—or, at least, heal the shame that binds it, err, or *bound it*—I guess. Be in the moment, 'cause that's all that counts, all there is.

"Did he buy that?" asks Sarah.

Well, not to begin with. But after a while, the trauma seemed to diminish. I think they got him on Paxil and Klonopin—and after a few weeks he appeared to improve considerably. Went back to work—and the peak episodes of anxiety and nightmares were fewer and farther apart in frequency.

"Cool. So he was all better just like that?"

No, I mean, c'mon, he was still pretty tweaked. But at least functional—and not suffering to the same extent. Feeling somewhat more in control, I suppose. I was told, for example, that there were still problems with, uhm, binge Bactine buying—and scissors.

"But vhat doez a problem vith ze Bakteen could it entail? I vould zink zat ziz indicates, no, zome continued mental devizit. After all, ziz poor man, he haz been abominated, *contaminated by ze underbelly of life'z more lowly evolved creatzures...ze kind zat vriggles zrough his feziz, no?"*

"Now, lemme get this straight," Sarah rattles. "So they've yanked the thing out, but he's still frying. Does he get better? What's the story?"

The story is that after a month or so, he definitely improves. Well, sort of. An essential component of the therapy has been to get him to accept the worm. To embrace it as something to which he is now intimately related. To feel close to the worm. To understand *its* point of view, if you will. To feel flattered, in a sense, that it chose *him*—not the guy down the street, not even the vice president of the United States. And to realize that one is bound to have issues of separation anxiety—that that's perfectly okay: postparticus wormus. And, they told him, any such longing to have the worm back inside, missing that "feeling of fullness," well, to understand that this is perfectly normal and will subside over time. That it always does.

"But zo maybe zen zay zhould've put it back een him, no? Zen he can have ze feelings of ze vullnezz all zat he vould like, ja? Or could zay give him inshted, zay, lotz of ze rice or how do you zay, ze bananaz, to make him ziz vull? Or vrom a different tact, maybe zome, vhat do you zay, depozitionariez, inzerted in ze ozzer end..."

Well, I think that at this stage everyone was well beyond this kind of...I mean, the idea was to promote some sort of acceptance of what had transpired. A worm type of zen, if you will. And anyway, to allow for this, they let him visit the thing in the lab, in—

"IN ZE BUCKET???! HE VENT BACK TO ZE BUCKET FOR ZE VULLNEZZ?!!?"

No, nooooo! Well, actually, yeah, he went back to the bucket, the pail, the specimen container, wherever it was they kept it. He had some sort of visitation privileges. Basically they were through with the particular tests they'd run—and by the way, he was given a clean bill of health. Apparently everyone was satisfied that it had not subdivided or that this wouldn't be an issue. So I guess they figured that permitting him to visit the bucket—for psychic mending, if nothing else—was a humane gesture. For worm closure, I suppose. But then it got out of hand. His mental state was making strides, but the emotional bond to the worm proved worrisome. He readily told all of his friends what had occurred, that he was *proud* of his worm—proud of how large and feisty it had become. Oh, he would insist, how they would love to see it swishing around in its dark blue little lab-pail. He named it Fred, because he once had a Dachshund named Fred. This was back when he was a kid, twelve years old. Found Fred wandering around an abandoned warehouse and, previously, had never had a pet—not a cat or a goldfish or a parakeet. But then, just three weeks after adopting the four-pawed orphan, the dog was mangled by a car. The front door of the house left open, Fred just fled—suddenly bolting out into the street. "Fred, come back," he had screamed, "FRED, COME!" But Fred did not come—and instead was mashed to a coarse pulp against the fire hydrant on Mr. Scarver's curb.

"*Ja, madged like a shkveezed puztchule...*"

Eventually, they even let him take the worm and the glop that it lived in—the entire specimen pail—they let him take it home! And he put it over the headboard of his bed, now irreparably carried away with this adopted worm son or daughter thing. But, on the other hand, he's functioning and back at work. And he seems to otherwise be calming down, with the shockwaves of the entire affair having more or less settled.

"*So, wait, like how long is this now after they'd yanked the thing outta his butt?*"

I think we're talkin' a couple of weeks.

"*And that's the end? He lives happily ever after?*"

"*Ja, I, of courze, vonder of ziz too—hiz vullnezz and zo vorth.*"

Well, here's how it all ends—it's rather grim.

"*Ja—grim. I can imagine grim.*"

Another week, ten days passes by. The entire episode, this whole thing, it's all beginning to look and feel, you know, very past tense. When...

"*When what?!! Gimme a break, don't even say it...*"

Well, I guess he came down with a head cold—or some sort of severe allergic episode. In any case, he was congested and sneezing and nose-runny, bad headaches. So they script him some decongestants and antihistamines—but all of this doesn't summon up considerable relief. So, what was it, oh, yeah that's right, he goes to the market and buys one of those giant nasal sprays. And he's sprayin' and sprayin'—until...

"*Until...?*"

Okay, so this time the wife, I guess we're all close enough to call her Helen at this stage—so Helen finds him face-frozen to the mirror back in the bathroom in the middle of the night (she was behind the shower curtain). And, uh, this time there's one worm coming out of the left nostril—it's about two or three inches long and another worm's jammin' out of the other nose hole, it's even larger. And, although it initially appeared to have been two distinct worms flapping around his now-paralyzed face, it turns out it was just one more giant worm—been living in his sinus cavities.

"*C'mon, you're making this up! How long was it living there? How did it get there? Was it part of the same worm from before?*"

This one was close to two feet long and had devoured almost half of the tissue lining the sinus. Supposedly this dark, moist, bacteria-laden cave ranks number one on a parasite's vacay wish-list. How it got there in the first place is anyone's guess. If it subdivided from the original worm you would think he'd notice the migration up through the esophagus and throat.

"Ja, you _vould_ zink zat. But zo now ve are zpeaking of ze vairmz in ze nose. More of ze vullnezz—more of ze orificial trauma. Ven vill eet all ztop, I azk of you? Ven do ve ztop ziz inzanity? Ze human body haz juzt zo many holes een it, if you vill. Holes zat can get to ze inzides of it. Ve could glue zem zhut—zen nossing could get een. But zat cannot be practical. Okay, zo zen ve could employ zertain chemical inzectizides, but zat may not be practical alzo.

"Ja, I zay good riddance. I underzhtand it all—ze vairms and ze vullness. Eef ziz man vants his vairms, I zay let him keep zem. Let 'em all keep zem. Zose who vant ze vairms—zay are eentitled to zem. Zat eez ze lezzon learned. And eet iz a cruel von."

OPEN MIC
JULY 1999

CLUB NOWHERE, SOMEWHERE, USA

Cover Charge: $10.00 (performers and guests not excluded)

Rules: One performance per sucker

Crowd: House is packed (Tuesday night); unlike most of these
affairs, audience sits attentive and all efforts are loudly
applauded. Far from the presence of a gong, onstage dude
can do no wrong. Let's take a peek:

White-haired white man, presumably sixty-something-ish, plugs
his wired acoustic guitar in the house PA, sets his ass down on a
stool, pulls the mic to his kisser, and he looks, well, way, way solemn.
There is going to be a pronouncement. It's coming. Yes, yes, here it
is, he says, "This is as relevant *now*, I think, as it was then. *Stop the
bombing!*" The buzzwords here, forecasting an unbearable four or
five moments of repugnant nostalgia to follow, are "this" and "then."
Because, you see, we are going to discover (there's no way out of this
[really]) how "this" equals "then." Are you ready? He is. Here he goes:

"White Biirrrrrrd..."

The fool's retro-yap has been opened for two seconds, maybe
three. The audience is silent with reverie—It's a beautiful day in the
early evening—so they think. You can see it—they are thinking this.
And he finishes to a standing ovation, expresses thanks, and once
again says, "*Stop the bombing!*" Yes, yes, that ubiquitous, infernal

bombing that just never, dammit, stops… Stop it. The stage clears quickly—peace-dude shuffles off, and what have we next? Big, crypto-Asian woman, late twenties. She places a boom box on a table, mic'd. She's wearing this gold-sequined blouse and tight black skirt that stretches even tighter over a tightly wide ass. She sweeps her fingers through her long black hair, tosses it back, turns on the *boom, b-b-boom. Booom, booom, booom. B-b-boom, b-b-b-b-b-b-booooooom!* On top of this clatter, she clutches the front-stage lead mic with a sweaty paw and gets into the rap:

> *"Mama Fortune Cookie! What they call me—*
> *But they don't know—what they can't see.*
> *You can open me up, and read what it say,*
> *But the fortune you get—not no fortune, my way!*
>
> *'Cause I this snaptrap don't hafta show no pussy.*
> *Mr. Massachusettes man, with ith your wrinkled old pecker,*
> > *yo, so wussy.*
> *I say stay away from Fortune Mama, Mr. New England man.*
> *I say stay away from my cookie, you understand?*
>
> *Mama Fortune breaks but she don't read*
> > *what you like.*
> *You snap her in half, but she no Far Eastern dyke.*
> *You pull out the paper to read what it say,*
> *And it say, 'Don't fuck with Fortune Cookie Mama that way.'*
> *That's what it say. Oh, Yeah. That's what it say.*
> *It always say…"*
>
> *…booom b-b-b-b-boom, booom, boom, b-b-b-b-booom.*
> *BOOOOOOOOMM!*

Wild applause from the Nowhere Club crowd ("Right on, sister," screams some petite but vigilant old-timer next to my table. She's shaking her fist in the air with abandon). Even the bouncer at the door has been moved (pumping airborne high fives). Mama Fortune Cookie trods off the stage with her traveling rap-PA. She receives a standing ovation, the kind that says "we've been profoundly moved— by something even more profoundly *heavy*—" as she saunters down the aisle and to the back of the crowd. My applause was directed more for, say, the Ed Wood via David Lynch nexus of this, but no matter. Whichever way you look at it, the *Fortune Cookie Woman Mama* a hit. At least this $10 per performer-chump scam offers some quality seconds of pubic hair angst.

Nonetheless, so far the duration of such quality is limited to Mama Fortune's one wild hog ride. Following this, we get a Jim Croce clone, some imbecile who can't let go of Boz Scaggs, and lots and lots of...rhythm and BLUES... Oh, is there anything else *worse* in the Western world than the requisite white-man, twelve-bar blues improv? But hey—$10 down at the door, you can be Eric Clapton or Eric Johnson or Eric Bloom or any of those lamebrain recycled Eric packages from Texas (or Eugene, Oregon) that churn out this crap ad-friggin'-nauseum.

But wait a minute; here comes something else. I mean, *somethin' ELSE*!

This tall-person hepcat with gnarled-out, curly black hair pulled back in a thicket-like pony-tail—more like a pony-*bush*. Has broad, black-framed spectacles, facial hair—lots of it. Calls himself—are you ready?—Mr. Black Top! Ho, ho. And it appears Mr. BT fancies being a beat-poet of sorts, got this new one, and he's passing out copies to us in the crowd so we can (presumably) read along. Wassit called? Why, this one's, uhm, titled "VEGETABLE GENITALS" (nice). He scratches his scruffy mane, clears his froggy throat, and starts:

"Uuhh, ladies and gents, may I have your attention? I wrote this next one, the one you have that I just handed out, when my bitch dumped me a couple of years ago. I was real, real depressed after that. And I made some serious life changes. I was tired of eating eggplant, if you know what I mean, and I also decided that I wouldn't clean myself, wouldn't shower for five months. I was searching for something I'd lost in that relationship, and that greedy, adulterous slut took all the money I had in the world. So I began to write. And write. I wear my heart on my sleeves, folks."

He clears his throat again. Then:

VEGETABLE GENITALS

Artichoke, I shall et,
Smoldering in your damp moisture,
My vegetable genitals
Like GIANT stalks of okra,
Once stir-fried in your WOK
With ginger and turmeric,
Curried, but now cold.

Silence (but, uhh, WOW!) then polite applause, people trying to suss out the hot haiku. Then Mr. Black Top clenches a fist in the air and offers that "the one on the backside of the page is a real barn-burner." He grooves the vibe, then launches the second one at us:

MY 2 ARMS

I GROW FROM THE GROUND
I SWING FROM THE TREES
I LAUGH IN THE WIND
HA HA HA!!
I FEAST ON A PLATE OF MOTTLED CLAY
WITH BLUE DUSKY MOLD GROWING ON ROTTEN,
SCABROUS TANGERINES
I SPOON THE PENICILLIN OF MY DREAMS
LIKE A SPONGEY BRAIN TUMOR FLOATING IN A
BOWL OF SLOW-COOKED OATMEAL

Gregg Turner

MY 2 ARMS
SURRENDER THE FRAGILE NIGHT
JUST LIKE THE VIETNAM WAR.

Holy Christ on a stick! My head was pounding, my ears scorched! Like a red-hot poker had been crammed into the recesses of my inner ear canal. We screamed for more: "Please. *More*, Mr. Black Top!"

He looked at us, me and two absolutely entranced partners in open mic crime. We were sitting at the table near the side of the room, eyes just riveted on this unlikely poetry slam hero. "Okay, here's another one," he beamed.

Another One

I got a new baby—and she's like a soft, sloppy doggy.

I got a new baby—and she's like a soft, sloppy doggy.

> Better than the last one,
>
> Maybe she's the new one,
>
> Or maybe just Another One.

I got a new baby—and she's like pistachio pudding.

I got a new baby—and she's no wrinkled raisin.

> Better than the last one,
>
> Or maybe she's the new one,
>
> Or maybe just Another One,
>
> Just another one.
>
> Yeah.

We stood up, saluted with the wildest of applause. We shouted, "ONE MORE, ONE MORE." Mr. Black Top, on his way off the podium, suddenly 180'd and obliged. "Okay," he nodded, "here's 'One More:'"

One More

Two More

Four Whores

Could this get any better?! The dude was clearly supercharged with most insightful fury and pathos. Equally humbled, we were, as he scurried off the stage. A smattering of applause, but that was all from Mr. BT. He gathered a bag together, put on a black wool cap, Lou Reed wrap-around shades, jaunted through the crowd (some pats on his back), and quickly vanished into the seeping dark of the packed house.

Next comes this gent from the back of the room. "Hi, I'm Addison."

"HI THERE, Addison," returns some other dude in the front. Addison checks him out, then asks us to clap clap clap. He stomps the beat on the floor of the stage. To the rhythm, he starts yowling his clap clap rap:

> "Baby, baby, I'm better than you.
> You humiliated me in front of your folks, I didn't know what to do.
> You stimulated me, you minimized me.
> You made me crawl to them on the floor, stripped down to my shorts,
> And what's more,
> I felt like a whore.
> Your dad swatted my 'hind
> As your mom stood behind,
> And you all laughed at me as my eyes went blind.
> Darkness in that room
> Ushered in the gloom
> That I felt for years,
> Hidden behind my tears.
> I love you, will always love you baby,
> But I can't get down with your mom and dad.

Addison finished and the room was pretty damn quiet. Then a few spotty good souls offered tenuous applause. The light on the stage dimmed for a couple seconds, then Addison ambled off. "Thank you, folks, I appreciate it." The room suddenly darkened and then a spotlight focused on some guy trying to move this along at a faster clip.

"NEXT," chirped this de facto master of ceremonies, "let's have a warm welcome for Little Louella!" LL perched down, strapped so tightly to a shiny, black acoustic GTR, on a stool with a single spotlight framing her meager specter. Started strumming. And strumming and so forth on and on. Huh? This went on for a while, then finally some lyrics:

> "I'm a prisoner of love.
> Oh, I'm a prisoner of love,
> And you've got the key,
> Baby, only you can set me free,
> But until then, I must be
> A prisoner of love.
>
> I'm a prisoner of love.
> Well, I'm a prisoner of love.
> Demons inside o' me,
> Angels, they cry for me.
> I guess I'll always be
> A prisoner of love..."

There is hushed, quite quiet reverence from the Club Nowhere clique craning their heads to pick up the stoic but still strident in mourning vokes emanating stealth-like from the PA. The melody is sweet, the remorse and pain veritably worn on Little Louella's cream-white sleeves. Then, suddenly quickly, from outta the blue, there's commotion. She's back to strumming and a-humming, but now there's rustling from the back of the place. Folks are standing up, someone's dancing down the aisle with a tambourine, closing in on the performer. Everyone's on their feet now; something is definitely up. It looks like, yeah, it looks like, could it be? Why, uh-oh, Mr. Black Top's back! He's now donning a—no, but yes! a fake *burka*, this big black shroud over his face and he jumps on the stage, banging the tambourine next to the singer. Was this part of the deal? Or maybe Mr. Black Top just couldn't help it and had to return to jump right in. He starts a-yappin', tambourine tappin', while Ms. Louella keeps strummin' strummin' strummin'. Over this, he starts a yelpin':

> "Don't be no prisoner of love, honey.
> Don't try God's patience above, honey.
> Don't sit in no jail cell, waiting for time to tell.
> Don't be no prisoner of luuuuvvvvve…
> *Why, Ah'lll love you, baby!*"

People were getting into this, some up on chairs, waving their fists, grooving to the pulse. LL was still lookin' down toward the ground hanging stubborn to the three-chord groove, and just as it occurs to us that alla the above is a bit over the Top, well, Mr. BT, he pulls out (yet) another piece of scribbled notes and lets 'er rip:

> "And now your brain hurts, baby.
> There's an octopus crazy, a real suction-monster, with tingling tentacles
> CLINGING onto your mind.
> Ohhh, issuing its poison, LEAD and strychnine.
> DEAD DEAD DEAD DEAD DEAD DEAD DEAD DEAD DEAD"
>
> …

The music just STOPS, everything STOPS, everything—crowd, performers, anybody who's anything STOPS and then just a truly righteous silence. When Mr. Black Top looks at us all and pulls off his shroud and BARKS OUT:

"ALIVE!"

Well, that's what it says here on the paper scraps supporting the copious notes I'd been scrawling all evening.

"Alive," he cried. Then the house lights blazed, and apparently the night was at its veritable end. No one would be the same for it. This was one open mic, like a soft, sloppy doggy, that sure wore out its welcome on less than a sour note (believe me, I've been to a lot worse).

DRIVE-BY

JULY 1997

It was 5:00 p.m. and I was horsing around with my two four-year-old Rotties, Pavlov and Joan. I had Pavlov pinned on his back with my mouth open around his throat. This was our favorite game, "Who's the Alpha?" We both faked our best growl as we replayed the moves we'd choreographed many times over in similar circumstances. It always resulted in a big lick for me and a kiss on a wet nose for him, and of course precipitous dog biscuits.

But this time the ending wasn't so congenial. Joan, eyeing this convoluted wrestling match, was muffling a bark or two from behind a nearby pillow. Turns out this had less to do with feelings of neglect or exclusion from "Alpha" and more to do with a juicy chew stick right behind my head on the floor as Pavlov and I were in the midst of dominance positioning. That's when things took an ugly turn. Joan suddenly pounced for the stick and Pav tried to intercept this effort—believing my head not to be an obstacle. My face was caught in the crossfire, top lip ripped apart up to my right nostril. Baaaaad Mr. Pavlov. Blood was spraying all over the place. Feverishly, I wrapped a towel around my face and headed for the local ER, *muy pronto*.

The incipient stage of ER registration, with the wound no longer ensconced in the beach towel's knot, was many times more than a nightmare. Hard to believe that much blood flows to and from the face. The towel was saturated, and now a swelling lagoon of expelled corpuscles puddled on the mat under the check-in window. Nonetheless, it was quickly apparent that expedience in patient processing was not a top-of-the-list concern here. After soliciting the necessary info, I was told to sit down in the waiting room and that I would be called "soon." "Possible to have another towel?" I asked.

"No, don't got no towels for the waiting room."

So I remained a fixture for what seemed like for-friggin'-ever, the bloody maroon towel shedding red cousin cells all over my shirt and pants as well. An older Hispanic gent finally sauntered by and did a double take, then ambled over slowly to inspect at a closer range. "Bro, what happened to you?"

Behind a mouthful of soggy, bloody towel cloth, I offered, very muffled, "Dog bite," assuredly less than discernible to the naked ear.

The old man looked at me, mystified, and asked again, "Bro, tell me what happened." Once again, I offer, mouth stuffed with blood-soaked fabric, "Dog bite." But again, I was certain that I was the only one comprehending this syllabic drenched description. Then, all of a sudden, the man's eyes opened w-i-d-e—he GOT it!

"Oh, no, DRIVE-BY, bro. That's just terrible. You should stay out of the west end of town, bro." And then he ran up to the check-in window and I saw him pointing at me, "DRIVE-BY, DRIVE-BY!"

The ER doors suddenly burst open, and I was escorted to a patient room (it seems I was unfamiliar with the correct password). They want to know if I was stabbed or shot. I tell them I was bit. They tell me that that's unusual in "gang-oriented combat." I try to explain that this was dog-related. And they reply that dog-retaliation is even more unusual in "gang-related reprisal," and by the way, what gang do *I* run around with? I say, "The Pavlovian Bell Ringers," and start laughing, as much of a chuckle as one could generate under the circumstances, but they don't get it and I pay the price 'cause you don't wanna laugh when your lip is split open and still spilling blood like a stuck fuckin' faucet.

After thirty minutes and more paperwork, the stitcher finally comes around. He's got a sewing needle and thread and a big hypo to shoot lots of lidocaine into my face. He confesses that he's color blind and so periodically asks a nurse to come over to monitor his "matching job." But we get along fine. We talk about my last colonoscopy, which was conducted without any pain meds by an Indian doc who had perfected a procedure feeding the colonoscope with a "jiggle technique" that he taught to all of his medical students. And in turn I got to hear a lot of rad stories about all sorts of sew-ups you wouldn't believe (a nose that had come off, a penile tear, a "full on scalping" as a crime of passion! I liked that one). So, all in all, not too bad a time.

And when I finally returned home, some four hours and sixteen stitches later, Joan and Pavlov had seemingly worked out their differences. Artifact of the crime scene, el chew stick, had been severed in half and both were munching their constituent parts up on the couch. I could see all of this through the front window as I pulled up in the drive-by, I mean driveway.

TWO-HEADED DAWG!

MARCH 1978

1. ELEVATORS AND DOG HEADS

In 1969 I met Darrell. I was a kid. He worked behind the counter at a liquor store around the corner where I lived. He was this crazy, older beatnik cat and we formed a quick bond, fanatic and crazy about anything Velvet Underground (back then outside of the Warhol circuit in New York the VU were relatively unknown—you could find new copies of the records in cut-out bins at pharmacies and grocery stores for thirty-nine cents). I'd been tossed out of a lot parties in subsequent years for replacing turntable samplings of "Hotel California" with "Sister Ray." Darrell was a bad influence. One day he looked at me and said, "You wanna hear something *really* on the edge? I think you're ready. There's this group called the 13th Floor Elevators—and they're just *out there,* man."

"Out there" was immediately appealing—and not long after that I gotta hold of their first record, *The Psychedelic Sounds of...* I was *way* out there, in over my head. The cover looked like a nightmare-swathed blotch of red and green wrapping paper with a Crayola pyramid eye in the middle. And the songs were these psyched-out, reverbed guitar stabbings behind this singer who shrieked and wailed like an electrically spine-charged Little Richard. And there was this bizarre bubbly noise that seemed to move seamlessly in and out of the sonic phrasing. If you closed your eyes and swallowed these sounds whole you were transported to some gnarled-out, frenzied, fevered peak. The songs could be beautiful and stridently nurturing ("Splash 1") and then on a dime aggressive, driving, and pulsating. I'd never heard anything like this. And there was this one song called "You're Gonna Miss Me" that was a diabolic beast. Like an off-the-track rock/roll tantrum that refused to quit or slow down. I played it ten times in a row. The singer's name was Roky, Roky Erickson. And *he* was way out there. Just no turning back now from the reverberations of this roller coaster ride. I was hooked. The Velvets were the gateway drug to something just as evil and wonderful and spiritually visceral.

ROger KYnard Erickson was born in Dallas in 1947 to Roger and Evelyn Erickson. Roger was an architect and civil engineer. Evelyn was an opera singer. Roky early on showed musical promise. He played piano at age five and then quickly picked up guitar. By all accounts he was charismatic and commanded attention in his formative years. He was the Mad Hatter in *Alice in Wonderland* when he was ten. When he was fifteen he formed a band in high school called the Spades. They put out a forty-five RPM seven-inch single, a crude, unpolished "You're Gonna Miss Me" with B-side "We Sell Soul," both tunes Roky penned. "We Sell Soul" became a regional hit of sorts. It wasn't long before Roky got mixed up with Tommy Hall, this mystical poet and LSD prophet (the "bubbly" noise weaving throughout the Elevators' songs was Tommy playing an amplified whisky jug). In 1966 he and Tommy formed the 13th Floor Elevators. "You're Gonna Miss Me" (as it appears on the *Psychedelic Sounds* LP) was rearranged with fiercer teeth than the Spades version and became a break-out, radio-charted hit in the southwest.

"Psychedelic" was the tip-off of trouble on the way. Tommy and Roky (as well as the rest of the band) salted their souls with nonstop excursions of acid and weed and became countercultural icons to a legion of likewise devoted, soul-searching, psychedelicized fans following the band in lockstep. Countless acid trips later, this madness eventually caught up with Roky. In 1968 he was diagnosed with undifferentiated schizophrenia. He had been busted for possession of one joint, which was a capital crime in Texas back then. Vicious bigwigs of Texas law enforcement had been after the band, looking to put a halt to the mounting popularity of the psychedelic rock outlaws who were suddenly gaining a crazy head of steam. Roky was the sacrificial lamb. He pleaded not guilty by reason of insanity and was sentenced to ten years in a psychiatric lockup in Houston. Here he was treated to electroconvulsive shocks. It's been told that Tommy and his wife Clementine actually assisted a few escape attempts from this hell—the payoff was his transfer to Rusk State Hospital where the shocks continued as well as a liberal dosing of Thorazine until his release in 1972.

During all of this, Roky continued to write poetry and music, eventually meeting up with Doug Sahm in 1974 after his release from Rusk. With Sahm, Roky tracked a new forty-five on the homegrown "Mars" label, "Two Headed Dog (Red Temple Prayer)" b/w "Starry Eyes," a gorgeous, dreamy ode to his wife, Dana. "Two Headed Dog" referenced the dog-head transplant experiments pioneered by the Russian scientist Vladimir Petrovich Demikhov in the 1940s and fifties. Demikhov's final double dog head creation occurred in 1959, which in turn inspired the monkey-head transplants of US neurosurgeon Dr. Robert White. Despite flimsy production, "Dog" had Roky wailing in fine form. Where once he mouthed the Tommy lyrics "Bedouin in tribes ascending, from the egg into the flower, alpha information sending, states within the heaven's shower..." in the Elevator's powerful anthem "Slip Inside This House," now he had his own rant: "Peace brought back brought back, relaxed be nyet brought back. Did you dry her out, wind her out like jerky? To me she's healed, don't tack!" Was this an ECT-inspired rant inherited from years of tortured imprisonment? If the tripped-out flower children were wondering where the sixties peace and love flower-power vibe from Texas had been hiding—it now was emerging in a whole 'nother costume. Roky Erickson had a new message: "I am an alien from Mars!"

He even went so far as to get a notary to certify such a thing, believing the shocks with which they, the ETs, were throwing his way, would vanish once he came out of his Martian closet. Apparently this worked.

2. **M-A-R-S**

In 1975, Doug Sahm was booked for a night at the Palomino club in North Hollywood. Eventually the Palomino would sponsor more mainstream pop and louder rock/roll events, but at this time the place offered a steady diet of bland country and western cotton-candy type acts and sounds. It really wasn't so much a musical venue as just a steak and beer chowder house where the ambient stage noise didn't get in the way of the food and drinks. By booking Sahm, the club was sticking its neck out a little bit. Sir Doug ("Mendocino") rocked out with more authority (than the usual crap that played there) and no apologies for this—but expectations were that his Tex/Mex good ol' boy Texas lineage and swagger wouldn't ruffle the feathers of the beer-swilling cowboy hats in attendance.

But me 'n' some buddies were hearing rumors that Sahm had actually brought Roky Erickson in tow to step in and Rok out with Sahm toward the end of the night. As unlikely as this sounded, we couldn't *not* take the chance that this might happen. So I threw on an old Elevators homemade T-shirt and traipsed down to the place with subdued expectations. I had long grooved to the Sir Douglas

Quintet's songbook, so even devoid of Roky this seemed to be worth the trouble.

Oh, boy—I just had no idea what I was in for! Sahm was traipsing between tables between the first two sets. I mustered the nerve to flag him down and asked, "Is Roky Erickson here tonight?"

Doug broke his stride and seemed incredulous that anyone would know this, let alone be hip to Roky. "Y'all know Roky?! Well, come here with me," he motioned. I followed him to a back room. Sitting at a long conference table was this scruffy-looking dude, unshaven and quite involved in explaining something very, very important to this woman perched right next to him inhaling his words. I waited to say hi, have him sign some vinyl I'd brought with me. He had this thick blue Sharpie and he was scrawling directly onto the table.

"NOW," he explains carefully to this woman, "mah mom was the first one who told me. Whaddaya call your mom?"

She furrowed her brow and offered, "Mother, mommy, uhh uhm..."

Roky retorts, "MA, right?" And he writes in dark blue, heavy ink, "M—A" on the table. He continues: "Now, what's the first letter of mah first name?"

The woman furrows again. She says, "Roky, so that would be 'R.'"

Roky nods seriously, "Yeah, R," and he adds R to MA, writes on the table, "M-A-R".

"Now," he throws it out, "what comes after R in the alphabet? S, right?" She nods, and now he adds S to the alpha string on the table: M-A-R-S. She gasps. And he shakes his head up and down and says, "Yeah, ah know. I couldn't believe it either the first time ah found out. Just scared the HELL outta me!"

So now it's past midnight and Sahm is halfway through his last set. He pauses briefly, looks out at the crowd, still a full house. "I'd like to introduce a good friend of mine who came with me all the way from Texas, Roky Erickson. He has some new songs and we'd like to share these with you." Everyone's lookin' around and this slightly hunched-over, hapless apparition is slowly making his way to the stage. He steps up, straps on a guitar, and goes to each amp and turns the volume to twelve! Suddenly he's not lookin' so hapless, now almost menacing. And he slams down the first chords, E-D-A-G, at ear-shattering volume, and starts screaming the first words of "You're Gonna Miss Me." The faces in the crowd are frozen, but when Roky launches into "Two Headed Dog," these expressions mutate to abject terror. The dude next to me, chewin' religiously on a piece o' meat, spits it out when Roky goes absolutely berserk, ranting how he's "been working in the Kremlin with a two-headed dog!" Honestly, I've seen some incredible things, witnessed some mind-blowing moments, but this is at the top of the list.

3. RAW MEAT 1978

Sunset over surf city, the soon-to-be somnolent solar furnace fading into the polluted layer of western horizon on the Pacific Ocean looked like an egg yolk peeking out of a plate of huevos rancheros with crimson salsa. If you look close enough you can see the latest version of Roky Erickson, in LA for a showcase gig at the Whisky a Go Go, pacing the length of his floppy motel flat in West Hollywood. It's room 111 ("that's 666 divided by six," he will offer), where Roky's handler Winston Taylor is likewise pacing up a storm between the two queen-sized beds. His pale apparition is scouring the carpet as he goes back and forth, back and forth, back and forth, back and forth. Roky's marching between two oppositely positioned mirrors on opposite-facing walls of the room. Both Winston and Roky have their arms clasped behind their backs, bent over, pacing, pacing, each synchronized to the same furious rhythm and immutable backbeat of angst. Roky's path, between the walls alongside the bottom of the two beds, is orthogonal to Taylor's march *between* the two beds. The paths cross, but the motion is parameterized so they don't collide. Before this never happens, some guy with only pants on from upstairs gallops past the open door of 111; this is when the pace-a-thon inside suddenly grinds to a halt. Roky snakes his head out the door, checking out the pants-only fugitive.

"Hey, Winston!" Winston keeps pacing. "Ah said, Winston, ah think the Antichrist just bit someone in the neck." (Winston is still pacing between the beds.) "Yeah, there's gonna be some blood spilled tonight, ghouls let loose and there's HELL to pay now—ah said, that poor guy, why, he had no blood left, that's why he was runnin' from his dead wife..." Winston nods several times, considering the gravity of the pronouncement, pacing, pacing, pacing.

Roky stares down the menu. It's dinnertime. He looks at the waitress. She has no clue at this particular moment why she will ultimately, and not too far in the future, be given a one-hundred-dollar cash tip (the obligatory gratis of dining with Roky). "What's this steak tartareee?" she is asked.

"You mean the steak tartare, dear?"

"No, ah mean the steak tar-tar-eee," he corrects.

"Sir, that's raw steak, it's uncooked."

Roky's eyes just BULGE OUT at this proclamation. At the top of his larynx, loud enough for the entire restaurant, he bellows: "Y'MEAN IT'S *RAW MEAT*? AH KIN ORDER *RAW MEAT* HERE?" His right hand is tightly gripping the fork. His forearm connected to his right paw is fully extended and stretched taut so that the fork is now an inch or two from the waitress's face, which is suddenly whiter than the tablecloth. Erickson's electric autoharp band member Billy Bill Miller, in black pants and a Daniel Webster tee shirt, stands up and spins three times in a circle and then sits down. Roky drops the fork and smiles at the waitress. "Well, ah think I'd like waffles, y'know?" Roky rotates in my direction, says, "I really do wish I could drink some Peruvian Borscht. Y'know, I wouldn't *shoot* anyone if I had a gun." He looks around to the other tables in the joint, as if there is even a reasonable chance that someone may be kind enough to hand over a gun. "Especially mah friends, ah'd never shoot mah friends if ah had a gun."

The original waitress has seemingly vanished in the moment. The concerned faces of a handful of staff and a disembodied chef's hat are visible peering around the corner wall. A new server saunters out; perhaps she's been briefed. Prompt immersion in the eye of the hurricane, she taps Roky on the shoulder, sighs, and engages the singer: "Let's see, now, you want, uhm...waffles? Is that right?"

He checks out the replacement, looks deadpan in the replacement's eyes, and after a moment's reflection, he shoots back, "Well, yeah, waffles. Waffles with blood from the manager's neck. Ah think that's what ah've been wantin' all day! Can we all have a party and drink blood?"

She takes a couple steps back and now suddenly is conscious that the entire place is riveted into Erickson's dinner order. Billy's twirling his fork, but just three times and stops. Winston, meanwhile, has been energized as if Dracula has called out code to Renfield. Roky looks like he's ready to pounce, but instead his eyeballs lock on the waitress, and he crows, "Someone here said y'all tear at a piece of *RAW MEAT*? Is the cook here, is he like a hungry dog, does he have RABIES, does the woofman cook the food, does he cook it *RAW*? Are we gonna eat the *MAYOR OF BEVERLY HILLS*?" Clearly Roky was just having the time of his life; it had been a while since I'd seen him in such high spirits; but waitress number two wasn't on an equal (or even reciprocal) wavelength. Really, all she had to say was, "Yeah, sure, Frankenstein is the sous-chef tonight, and we just offed the mayor and y'all can chew on the arms and legs," but she missed the bait and instead looks over to Billy. But he isn't ready to order either; he's explaining his top-secret idea for a brand-new kid cereal to me, then ultimately to the whole table.

The server conspicuously diverts attention from Roky, looking for anyone prepared to order food. She's now trying even harder to ignore that Roky has apparently dumped about twenty or thirty packets of sugar and a whole container of cream into his coffee cup, which, as a result, has spilled over into a precipitously huge puddle on the table, streaming down to the floor to form an even larger caffeine and cream lagoon. The server's still working on Miller, perhaps hoping his commitment to a food decision could possibly bellwether the rest of the troop. But that doesn't pan out. Billy's now dialed into a conceptual nexus far beyond the restaurant's menu. No, the waitress standing there with bottomless patience to move this part of the dining process along is quickly factored out by Billy. He's busy ranting about his favorite horror flicks, *The Colossus of New York* and *The Killer Shrews*. Roky and Winston dig this truly, acknowledging the weight of the filmic art with serious nods as autoharp's pronouncement plays out.

The energy at the table is mounting. Finally, Roky looks up to the waitperson and just WAILS at the top of his larynx: "HAVE THEY COOKED THE MAYOR'S BRAINS YET? WHERE'D Y'SAY THE HUMAN SLAUGHTERHOUSE WAS? AH THINK AH NEED TO GET A MEAT CLEAVER, ONE DRENCHED IN BLOOD, Y'KNOW, SO AH KIN EAT A WHOLE HUMAN SKULL TONIGHT. YEAH, ROTTING BONES FROM THE CEMETARY. BUT AH WOULDN'T CHOP ANYBODY UP, LIKE THE FAMILY SITTING OVER THERE AT THAT TABLE, THE ONES EATING HUMAN EYEBALLS OR ANYTHING. AH MEAN, AH'M NOT THE CANNIBAL THAT ATE THEIR MISSING CHILD. AH SAID IF AH HAD A BUTCHER'S

KNIFE, AH WOULDN'T DO ANYTHING AH'D REGRET. MEAT HOOK ONE! ROKY!

"OKAY, NOW AH'M REALLY HUNGRY, WHEN KIN AH GET MAH FOOD?!"

4.   HAUNTED HOUSE RECORDS

Are those *sirens* we hear peeling down Sunset Boulevard? Five twenties are quickly left on the table and the entourage evacuates the restaurant, piling into the car and back to the Tropicana motel. Everyone's bushed, 'cept of course Roko, who's now on infinite repeat about wanting to go to the all-night "Haunted House Records" (he means Tower Records, then the mega emporium of retail music chains). He says he's looking for the soundtrack to the Broadway musical, *Gurgling Sounds That Vampires Make*. He's also looking for—he has this written down on some scrap of paper—another musical production *The Hideous Sun Demon That Bit Off the Mother's Head*, though he's not entirely sure this "musical" actually made it to Broadway—or, for that matter, even the record store (*"It may be too far out, man, for even the Haunted House Records. They might have had one copy, but the police chief probably bought it so that no one else could hear it. He goes to all the stores and buys all the copies so people won't believe it exists"*).

The important thing is that if ANY store might have it, it'd be Haunted House Records on Sunset Boulevard. In fact, this will be the ONLY store, the "only one in the world" that could have it in stock. It might be the one place that wouldn't let the police in to buy the only copy. "Man, it's a really horrifying musical, almost a comedy, but it's really horrifying 'cause when the demon bites off the mother's head, it's like a geyser erupts and when that happens, most of the audience is just real horrified 'cause THEN they understand that the mother won't be able to have any more babies." Manager Craig, noticing how amped up Roky has become, says it's okay to go to Haunted House Records on Sunset Boulevard, in fact, here's some money and why don't both of you go look for some groovy show tunes? But probably a good idea to stay away from that *Killer Bee* movie. Promise? I promised.

The 11:30 showing of *The Swarm* was the only one not sold out so that's the one we went to. Yeah, I know I promised, but you don't understand what it's like when Roky wants to do something really bad. And when that something's a horror movie on his A-list, there's just no way to divert the obsessive focus. Plus, we struck out with any type of gurgling sounds at Haunted House Records. When Roky asked the manager for the second time to check if the one copy of *The Hideous Sun Demon That Bit Off the Mother's Head* had already been purchased, the guy nodded and wryly cracked that "maybe you should give Charles Manson a call." Erickson's eyes opened W-I-D-E at this suggestion. He looked plaintively at me, thinking, "CAN WE?" but I deflected and told Rok that Manson's not a local call. Which, incredibly, convinces him that this now is a cold trail ("Oh, right, he probably lives too far away to be called on the phone").

So, uhm, now we're sitting in the very first row of the theater ("that's where you can see all the things they don't want the rest of the people to see") when the first swarm takes place ("just don't go to that killer bee movie"), not ten minutes into the flick. The celluloid frozen face on the screen is now shrieking in bee-stinger agony. I look over to note that Roky's silhouetted profile has become equally transfixed with immediate and appreciable TERROR. It's the kind of viewer empathy that peaks and crashes down on only the tuned-in and sensitized psyches, the ones who can dial the right station to receive the right message (that's only broadcast to the front row that all the rest of the people, greater than or equal to the second row, can't hear or see). Angry, hive-hideous psycho-insects are at any moment gonna fly out of the screen and at us—no, at *him*. Roky looks over at me, and whispers, now almost afraid to be marginally conspicuous (killer bees watching), "Hey man, y'think there's more than *fifty thousand stingers* in that guy's face? Why don't they just go all the way up his nose and *sting his brains out*?" Tough questions to resolve.

5. **THE BRAIN HERNIA**

I pulled into the Tropicana parking lot the next morning. The plan was to shuffle the band and Roky to a local radio station out in Pasadena for a live lunchtime interview. The DJ who set this up got it—hip to Roky and all the songs. And he dug the 13th Floor Elevators, so this looked to be a bona fide opportunity to hype the Whisky show that night. But there now appeared to be some type of, uhm, problem. I could tell right when I pulled into the parking lot next to Roky's room that an "issue" had developed. Autoharp was pacing on the pavement outside, and he nervously acknowledged my presence when I opened the car door.

"Uhhh, you'd better wait here for a moment. Uhhhh, it's just not goin' too well in there." In where? Uh-oh. I started to get the picture, though the picture I imagined could only pale to the real picture that was unraveling inside the motel room. Roky had looked a little funky when I dropped him off after *The Swarm* last night ("*probably best not to go to that killer bee movie, Okay?*"), but it had been a long day, it was almost 4:00 am, and he was still sorta bummed about the dead-end at Haunted House Records. Besides, when he got out and went to his room and looked back at me and said he had a groovy time and, "AH GUESS YOU REALLY **ARE** MAH HORROR PAL, AREN'T YOU? WE'RE PRETTY HORRIFYNG TOGETHER, AREN'T WE?"—well, my heart turned to microwave cheddar cheese. You just cannot get a higher compliment and expression of bonding and affection from Roky Erickson than being designated a kindred "horror pal." But while I slept well that evening, more than psyched by the accolade, Roky wasn't having such a good time. Not a good time at all: seems *The Swarm* came into his room through the ventilation system.

When I finally sauntered into the motel room, manager Craig and guitarist Duane Aslaksen just looked shot. They were wearing expressions halfway between "we've seen this all before, no big deal," and "we haven't seen ANYTHING like THIS before, what the heck happens NOW?" The air was thick with silence. Roky was sprawled out on the bed. As I meandered alongside to see what the deal was, he picked up: "Hey, man, hey, there, y'all are probably the only one who kin understand what happened—we're ghoul brothers, so ah think you'll see." I backed off a few steps. "Remember when we saw that horrifyin' killer bee movie last night?" Craig fired me a quick look of death ("*probably best not to go to that killer bee movie, okay?*"). "Wal, when I was sleepin' they came through the vents over there and ah had to run for it." The bathroom, as I nervously looked sideways, appeared more than lopsided. That's where at least one vent must have been located. Roky plaintively continued: "Now, ah haven't told many people about this, but a long time ago ah had a stomach hernia. Mah guts spilled out and they had to find a doctor who could sew 'em back in. But last night—why, ah had a BRAIN HERNIA. Y'see, ah was outside and mah brain just fell on the ground, right out there. But ah was real lucky, there was a woman behind me when this happened and she was a surgeon. So she put it back in mah head and sewed it up and so I expect to live. But, uhhh, ah won't be able to sing anymore. Ah can't sing tonight when we're gonna play, 'cause mah brain could fall back on the ground. In fact, ah can't sing anymore, ever, at all."

"Can you do interviews?"

"Uhmm, why, no, ah can't."

Was it the brain surgeon in the night who then telepathically communicated that her sutures in his head could actually withstand the rigors of doing the KROQ-AM interview at noon? Or maybe it was the lure of the stuffed "woof" that he spotted in the Witch's Shop on Santa Monica Boulevard en route to the radio station. A deal was struck, and no sooner than you could say John Agar (*The Brain from Planet Arous*), Roky was hugging this giant stuffed woof in the backseat, his recently herniated brain now apparently enjoying a second wind.

The DJ at the station wasn't the one who was supposed to be there; that guy had botulism or something. The substitute had absolutely no inkling as to what this was about or what was going to go down. "So, Roky, it says here that you were the lead singer and songwriter of Texas's cult band the 13th Floor Elevators. We just heard the song "You're Gonna Miss Me," wasn't that a big hit for you guys?"

"Well, yes, it was."

"Yeah, well that's a pretty rockin' tune there, you wanna tell all our listeners how that came about?"

"Well, yes, I would... See, that's about when the Fahr Demon eats the little baby, and uh, then Frankenstein comes out and eats the baby's head. But then he, uh, vomits and all these maggots come out, and then he eats the vomit and the maggots and the maggoty babities' head...and starts vomiting again. It's a real scary song, 'Stand for the Fahr Demon' is."

The DJ has his hand over his mouth, suddenly nauseated. He barely was able to squeeze out encouragement for Roky to promote the show at the world-famed Whisky a Go Go. "Wal, y'see, last night ah had a brain hernia," the singer tells the greater LA listening audience on live AM radio. "Mah brain fell out into the mud, but there was a surgeon who was standin' behind me and she sewed it back in mah head. It was really horrifyin', man...

Ah guess ah didn't think ah could sing tonight, ah was gonna tell everyone not to come out, 'cause of mah brain hernia. But, uhh, ah think I kin sing again, the surgery is feelin' real good now, so ah don't think there's gonna be any trouble. *Frankenstein*! *Murders in the Rue Morgue. From Hell It Came.* This is Roky. Ah said, I wouldn't drink your blood if you were mah friend. Ah said, FUNERAL HOME! Ah wouldn't shoot anybody if ah had a gun!" Billy and Winston had been pacing, but by the end of all this, they owned the knowing wavelength that apparently the surgery had indeed gone well and Roky was back. In fact, this might have even been one of the best interviews he'd ever done.

6. JOE MEEK

The Aliens were Roky's backup band in the late seventies. Unto themselves they were a devilishly spirited, ferocious sonic tour de force that platformed and locked in Roky's songs. The rhythm section (drummer Jeff "Mule" Sutton and bassist Morgan Burgess) pulsated a glowing, neon-like anchor to drive the beat, but man, oh, man, the Aliens had two other superstar not-so-secret weapons. Lead guitar Duane Aslaksen, who looked like a young Keith Richards, was blinding fast and furious with melodic scales and dynamic riffing. Boy, was this guy great. One of the unsung guitar heroes of the twentieth century. No exaggeration. Duane could play the tail off the donkey; he accentuated Roky's barre chord patterns while adroitly juxtaposing his lead licks with the vocal melodies. Aslaksen's interludes and lead accents were astutely intelligent—they anticipated and slyly magnified Roky's rhythm hooks.

Then there's the autoharp guy, Billy Bill Miller. I'm at a loss really to describe the extent of Miller's prodigious wizardry attacking this instrument. He can sound sweet and even sourly dissonant, or he can growl on a dime and sound like a demonic splatter of

Jimi Hendrix and Lou Reed! He plays the zither unlike anyone I've heard—really more like a guitar with unflagged and punishing chops. When you think autoharp, you think of your music class in second grade: "Michael row the boat ashore..."—accent chord strums on "row" and "shore"—you get the picture. Miller turns the harp on its head, a satanic spawn of sound that is expelled with one thousand hellish decibels that dog-barks back to the rest of the band. This is not a peace and love presentation of the instrument. He wears it fastened tightly to his body and scratches at the strings. Sometimes with a scalpel. The crazy sound is both heavenly and unearthly apocalyptic.

Billy has an outstanding government patent for a kid cereal called "Oswald Crunchies" (cheerios with crosshairs in the middle and a "toy gun premium in every box!" he will tell you). He once owned a humongous pet lizard (a Tegu) that he would take for neighborhood walks on a dog leash when he lived in Mill Valley, California. Miller is a rabid fan of early British sixties musical producer Joe Meek (Meek recorded and produced the Honeycombs ["Have I the Right"], came up with the mega hit instrumental "Telstar," and is often described as the British Phil Spector). And Billy also ingests ominous waves of mid-twentieth century sci-fi celluloid extravaganzas like director Jacques Tourneur's *Night of the Demon* and *I Walked with a Zombie*. Meek, a historically unstable bright light, ultimately suicided. Billy Miller is still going strong. I'll let him fill y'all in.

"My career has been *plagued* by the fact that nobody ever knows that all these sounds, the ones you hear all the time in our songs, are made by the autoharp..."

For example, that eerie, ghostly wailing sound in "Burn the Flames" is your autoharp?

"Yes, that's right. It is played with a scalpel. This is necessary to cut the notes out. More than I could do with other slide devices. For most ghostly wailing and other sounds I use my fingers, but on this song it has to be the scalpel—just like at the end of 'Sputnic' ['Spelling Your Theory, Alien I Creator']."

What is the "Claw"?

"The Claw is a mechanical assembly on the back of the autoharp—two metal claws which attach to the metal bar that is part of that thing that I wear which is secured with a strap. There's a stainless steel shield that is covered in black velvet which keeps the Claw from digging into me as it swivels and attaches itself to the bar. The claw is powered by elastic. It allows me to play with more power by adding extra leverage. It also allows the autoharp to be worn like a "side-arm," y'know, like a six-shooter. When people ask me who my greatest influence is, as a musician, well, I always tell 'em—Chuck Conners."

You possess a patent for the Claw, is this correct?

"Yes."

You're an inventor, then?

"Yes. I created an electric spacesuit for large lizards which allows them to go out for walks in the snow. Walking them on a leash is no longer for warm climates only, but it's an expensive luxury for the pet owner who wants to take Lizzie along on ski trips."

Ah, you're sort of like a mad scientist?

"That's it. Roky's *always* has been in the company of mad scientists. First Tommy Hall [lyricist and jug player with the Elevators], then me."

I've heard you're eccentric. Is this fair?

"I'm afraid to touch metal (due to an excessive amount of personal electricity). And I have a compulsion to overturn rocks to see what creatures hide underneath. I have a fear of germs and mushrooms."

Director Jacques Tourneur and British music producer Joe Meek seem to be particularly important icons to both Miller and Roky. Billy elaborates:

"Tourneur was Roky's cinematic guru and mentor, along with being North America's greatest director. He's the one responsible for *Night of the Demon, Cat People,* and *I Walked with a Zombie.* It's all in the trees. A substantial part of the Roky mythos is typified by lines like "a death to life séance and ghostly powers all the time," which can be found in the works of Tourneur—seemingly as obsessed with Wood Spirits as David Lynch in *Twin Peaks.*

"The 'séance' referred to by Roky in 'Night of the Demon' is, in fact, conducted by the character (in the movie) 'Mr. Meek.' Are these points of connectivity mere coincidence or paranormal occurrences? It's hard to believe that Tourneur could have actually been aware of Joe Meek in 1957 when *Night of the Demon* was released. But synchronicity follows Roky and the whole Aliens clique—right down to the Buddy Holly connections.

"Tourneur used a telephone to the most frightening effect ever in 'Night Call,' the only *Twilight Zone* episode that he ever directed. It was about a lonely old lady receiving phone calls from a dead line during a storm. The dead phone line eventually is found to be down in a cemetery—laying over a grave. Communication lines laying over graves and radios that can tune in the dead are the type of subjects which are finally mainstream in the mass consciousness fueled by moguls like the late mega-radio host Art Bell. But Roky was fully aware of this type of reality since he was old enough to speak. You have the three-year old Roky stirring controversy in Sunday School by his defiance of death at the same time as the thirty-year-old Joe Meek recorded the screams of ghosts in graveyards.

And these connections—I've just scratched the surface.

"Joe Meek had hundreds of songs that were not far off from the Aliens' sounds and many that were not far removed from the Elevators' sounds. But it goes a lot further than just the sounds and production. The themes that Joe seemed to favor closely paralleled a large part of Roky's themes as far as songs go. Roky wrote 'Sputnic' as his answer to 'Telstar.' Roky and Joe both had songs of the title 'Night of the Vampire.' Even more ironic—and this is just flat-out crazy-strange—Duane Aslaksen's guitar intro on Roky's 'Night of the Vampire' is note for note identical to Joe's song of the same title. Duane had absolutely NEVER heard that song when he composed the intro. Lately, I've wondered if maybe Roky spoon-fed Duane that intro melody. Maybe all these years I incorrectly assumed it was Duane. But if Duane did in fact compose that intro, it's more bizarre synchronicity between Joe Meek and Roky and the Aliens."

7.   **HOT CARS**

Live radio interviews with Roky were always a kick. There was the time he was the featured guest on popular KSFR FM in San Francisco. The Sex Pistols were coming to town to play Winterland (which turned out to be a dreadful sonic, out-of-tune sludge fest, their very last gig). Guest DJ Howie Klein, local Frisco punk rock scene maker at the time and head of 415 records, asked Roky on air if he had a favorite Sex Pistols song. Roky thinks for a minute, then proclaims, "Why, yes, ah do, ah got it, yeah, it's 'Hot Cars.'" We all crack up (no such Pistols tune, of course).

"Yeah, that's a good one, my favorite too!" chortles Howie. But then there really *needed* to be a song called "Hot Cars," so Metal Mike

Saunders and I jumped on the calling—"Hot Cars" appeared on the debut Angry Sams record, *Inside My Brain*, in 1980! But the really mind-blowing factoid is that just a couple years ago—fast forward to 2019—I'm checking out YouTube movies, and there's this godawful 1956 B-movie (is there such thing as a C-movie?) about carjacking and insurance fraud called, you guessed it, *Hot Cars!* (the same filmmaker issued another masterpiece of celluloid genius, *Stakeout on Dope Street*, two years later).

8. GRAPEFRUIT SEED

After the Whisky gig on the night of the KROQ interview, at around two in the morning, we ventured down to Cantor's Deli on Fairfax to take Roky out for a nosh. We're seated at our table, and glasses of water are served all around. Guess whose glass happens to have a grapefruit seed in it? Right. And he's just staring at it, really not saying anything for the longest time. The waitress comes by, and now he's voicing greater concern.

"Is there something I can help you with?" she asks.

Roky's still fixated on the glass of water, but replies, "Well, ah, it seems ah got a seed in mah water." The waitress checks out the glass, apologizes, and offers to bring a new glass, seedless of course. But that doesn't fly 'cause Roky's consumed maybe half a milliliter of the water, so in other words, he's ingested some of the seed water. The waitress assures him, looking at us for backup, that the seed assuredly has been through the dishwasher so, y'know, it for sure is a CLEAN seed, no need to worry about health issues drinking seed water. That appears to placate Roky for a few minutes, but just as suddenly he bounds up from the table holding the glass with the grapefruit seed, and shrieks, "Ah know what this is, it's not a grapefruit seed, it's the goddamn DEMON seed, I drunk the DEMON SEED." And with this pronouncement, the anxiety springloads a psychic tsunami. Deli diners at adjacent tables looked like they were gonna bolt before they were served demon seed water as well, so the management not so warmly encourages us to take off ("get the fuck outta here and take him with you back to the Hollywood Hills—or wherever he comes from," we were told). One hundred dollars left on the table and we make tracks.

9. LELAN ROGERS

I finally make it home from the grapefruit seed fiasco, pretty wrung out. The next day there's a promotional party—hyping Roky's premier solo LP release, *The Evil One*, on the Sunset Strip at *Crawdaddy* magazine's headquarter.s [The original release of the record was on the British CBS label and it was an astounding document of comeback. The sonic production was incredible, and the impeccable list of indelible tunes on the record included "Stand for the Fire Demon," "Don't Shake Me Lucifer," "It's a Cold Night for Alligators," "The Interpreter," "Two-Headed Dog," "I Walked with a Zombie," and "White Faces" *("friends with the beast, because of sharp teeth.")*]

Lelan Edward Rogers (1928–2002) was the eldest of a family of eight and Kenny Rogers's older bro. He was a producer, musical exec, and once-in-a-while hustler, eventually accruing local notoriety with Houston's International Artists record label where he was signed on to produce the 13th Floor Elevators in 1966. Here he also produced and managed some of the more peculiar and innovative Texas local musical outfits which included the Bubble Puppy ("Hot Smoke and Sassafras") and the Red Krayola (featuring Mayo Thompson—Lelan discovered the Red Krayola at an outdoor shopping mall; later on, at a gig in Berkeley, the band mic'd the drippings of a massive block of ice on a snare drum as their percussive metronome). Lelan produced all four of the IA-released 13th Floor Elevators records (*The Psychedelic Sounds of*, *Easter Everywhere*, *Live* (which wasn't—just outtakes and leftover unrecorded tracks with applause dubbed in), and *Bull of the Woods*). Lelan (known as the "Silver Fox") managed the band (as well as anyone could manage the acid-scourged upside down circus of the group) and wound up in over his silver-foxed head procuring ginormous quantities of weed and psychedelics— particularly for studio session tracking of the band's records. There are countless crazy stories chronicling such escapades, like the time that lead guitarist, Stacy Sutherland, brought a pet spider monkey to the studio sessions of their second mind-blowing record *Easter Everywhere*. "They kept dosing that monkey with LSD and it spent most of the time swinging around with its head in the speakers," Lelan would tell me later on. "Then it would jump down to crap all over the sound board, and toss turds at everyone in the room."

I'd written a piece for *Bomp* magazine in 1975 on Lelan and International Artists and all the loopy Texas bands that Lelan produced and released on the label back in the last half of the sixties. This article apparently caught his attention and he reached out and asked me to work for him. He wanted to reissue the whole IA catalog, all twelve records. These were fetching big bucks as sought-after collector's items, particularly the Elevators LPs. Lelan, not one to let prospective loot slide through his hands, brainstormed the idea to release a box set of the IA catalog. There was a Bekins warehouse in Encino, California, where he had all the master tapes and vinyl stored. The game plan even involved adding to the catalog and releasing an International Artists LP #13 (go figure!), which would be a double record set offering previously unreleased IA singles and unheard outtakes from the Elevators, Red Krayola, Lost and Found, and other IA label mates.

So in 1977 Lelan appropriated a suite of offices high up in the Century City (financial area not far from UCLA) twin towers. Here he ran two incongruous enterprises. The first involved putting together the IA box set and creation of the IA #13 double disk (to be entitled *Epitaph of a Legend*)—that was my charge. The other operation was a rhythm 'n' blues project—he'd scout for R&B and blues artists ostensibly looking to record and issue vinyl. I really was clueless what this involved. I was obsessively working the IA side of the business. Turned out that the only blues Lelan had up his sleeve was a rip-off scam—he'd find doctors and lawyers in Oxnard and Ventura (California) who needed a bigtime tax write-off. So he'd record these R&B folk and sell the ownership, publishing, and rights to these "investors." I have no idea if and for how much these musicians were compensated, but the records were never pressed nor released, the resting place of the master tapes (mixdowns not necessary!) in deep storage...somewhere in Oxnard or Ventura in Dr. Johnson's medicine cabinet.

As you can imagine, these performers and songwriters were less than thrilled to discover their songs and sounds had disappeared into a vinyl black hole. I was wandering around Lelan's side of the office suites one day, and I caught him frantically bolting to the private bathroom down the hall. What the...? He snapped the bolt and locked himself securely inside as three of the *California Blues Machine* gave chase, two waving pistols in the air. Boy, they were PO'd. "Where the fuck are you, Lelan?" they screeched as they frantically tromped down the hall past his secured lavatory hideout. This little psychodrama played itself out a few times in various shapes over the two years we were in business. The private bathroom hide-spot usually worked, ultimately security would remove the varmints, and Lelan would emerged unscathed.

The most lopsided (and tragic) incident occurred on August 24, 1978. I was walking down the hall from Lelan's office when he yelped at me to come sit and dig the phone call his secretary had on hold. It was Bunny Sutherland, Elevator lead guitarist Stacy's wife. (Stacy lived a precarious life—he was a more than amazing guitar talent, just so fluid and nuanced, but drugs and cop hassles inevitably brought him down. There was the time onstage, e.g., when his brain's cerebral folds were swathed with a liberal Elevators' party pack of potent acid and he hallucinated his beard to be a humongous blood clot and ran off into the rafters.) Anyway, before Lelan picked up the call on hold from Bunny (he wanted to surprise me, knowing what an unrepentant Elevators' fan I'd been), he shouted to me, "Listen, man, sit down—you won't wanna miss this: I have Stacy Sutherland's wife on the line!" But he wasn't ready for what was gonna go down. He switched to speaker phone. Bunny was moaning and just shrieking, "Lelan, it just went off, I dunno, I dunno—Stacy's bleedin', he might be dead!!" Lelan's eyes erupted, bulged, and opened wide, his face whiter than a whiter shade of pale. She kept screaming and crying, and Lelan wrapped his forearm over his mouth and ran to the bathroom. She was frantic. I ran after Lelan. And Stacy ultimately left the building, the victim of this apparently "accidental" shooting.

Which brings us back to Roky at the *Crawdaddy* party. Lots of folks mingling. I'd been working for Lelan for close to a year at that point and I talked him into coming by and saying hello to Roky. The two hadn't crossed paths in close to a decade. Roky ambled toward him. He looked at Lelan. "Oh, mah god, Lelan. How come you're not dead yet?!"

Lelan turned red, hugged Roky, and offered that he loved the new songs. "'I Walked with a Zombie'" is just gorgeous, Roky, a really clever turn on 'Stand By Me,' when did y'all write that?"

Roky thought for a moment. "Ah put that together when mah mother ate some alligator meat, y'know, and then the insects came out of her nose."

Lelan Rogers passed away in 2002.

Roky Erickson died at age seventy-two on May 31, 2019.

A CUP OF PUS
JUNE 2002

Primary colors are blue, yellow, and red (blood pus).

A story comes to mind (I shall proceed like a rabbi offering metaphor). It's called "A Cup of Pus." A painter friend of mine who used to live in Taos (New Mexico) found encroaching urbanization of this tourist stop in the northern part of the state too much (lately) to take from the sleepy little hippie hollow that (originally) lured his mind and bones from Los Angeles twenty years ago. So he up and moved an hour from Taos to an even sleepier little painter community called Tres Piedras (not to be confused with the *Monster of Piedras Blancas*, who [the monster] decapitated the heads of village fisherpeople and tossed the freshly severed caps on the iceberg and romaine in the produce section of a mom-and-pop grocery!). Here, he, uhm, painted. For quite a while. But then after some time he hit a creative brick wall—wasn't at all pleased with the textures of the paints he was using, nor terribly fond of paint, per se, as a medium. Looking for a "different viscosity," he would say. That's the end of the story.

Now I'll tell you the beginning. Oh, I'd say it was about eight months ago, there were two nieces visiting from Petaluma, California (egg capital of the west). Niece number one was maybe about twelve years old. Niece number two, let's say she was fifteen. Now the arrangement they'd worked, so as not to interfere with uncle's creative juices on canvas, was that they'd hang out, the niece people, in the main house, catch the tube and internet, video games too (not much else to do or explore in Tres Piedras), while Uncle logged artist time in the studio down the driveway. At night they'd all be together, tell ghost stories, and drink coffee! That's the beginning of the story.

Here's the middle part: as alluded to earlier, he'd been on the clothrag for many months trying to figure out the suitable paint-medium, searching through the desert brush for wild solvents, cholla juice, or reasonable facsimile. And in the process he incurred a nasty cactus wound, which, in turn, cherried up to a plum-sized boil, purple on the outside, oozing from the inside. Astute he was, and in this state of astuteness, he began draining and irrigating the abscess into an old tin cup—that is, he sampled and collected the dead white-cell excess. The viscosity was good, felt right immediately on both the small and large brushes—strokes to the canvas were good too. The only problem was the quantity harvested from the singular wound just couldn't deliver the amount needed to complete the still-life on which he'd been laboring. So this is why, perhaps, over a period of time, he suffered continued misfortune with stray cactus needles, but then this provided for lots more viscosity—and when he wasn't experimenting with combos of different wound secretions, he'd store the excess in the refrigerator in the kitchen (yet more viscosity).

Which brings us to the second middle part of the tale: the nieces were hungry one day; video-game calorie requirement demands copious treats. Search and Destroy mission to the fridge scored points for leftover chocolate cake, but they DID NOT LIKE AT ALL the small tin custard cups of Crème Brûlée next to the milk. Why on earth didn't he use sugar or honey—or at least maple syrup? WTF.

Gregg Turner

DREAMS
SEPTEMBER 2019

Ring.

"Hi. I'm trying to reach Gregg Turner."

"Yeah, that's me."

"Well, apparently there's been some clerical error. This is the graduate office at Claremont Graduate University. It appears somehow we miscalculated your total course credits for your doctoral degree. You're one course short, three credit units, of the amount you need to finish."

"What? That was ten years ago. I marched onstage, received my diploma."

"We apologize for the mistake, but your degree is no longer valid. You need to complete three more credits at the high-school level. You apparently never received credit for the Introduction to Criminology class listed in your transcript. You need to take this over again."

"That's ridiculous. I got an A- on my term paper on Albert Fish, the Cannibal."

"Well, we don't have a record of this. We checked with your high school transcript and it's not showing up. Your school is running this course again, right now, and you need to go back and enroll and pass the class. As soon as you complete this, your course requirements will be satisfied and your doctoral degree will be finalized."

School bell rings. Final exam at 11:00 a.m. for Intro to Criminology course in fifteen minutes. Room 203, Everett Hall. That's on the other side of the school. I sprint past the baseball field, past the administration building—finally reach, outta breath, Everett Hall, bolt up the stairs to second floor. Room 203. Note on the door: Final exam moved to room 542. Aargh. Lunge up the staircase, three more flights, room 542. 10:50 a.m. Note on the door: Final exam now in room 510. What? Run down to 510. Note on the door: FINAL EXAM NOW IS IN…HELL, proctored by the fuckin' devil. Uhh, look on my watch, five minutes to get there. I think I know how and where. Run to the dumpster behind the softball field. I smell the stench. Big green trash dumpster, brush aside rotting sandwich meats and dead cat. Lots of flies. Jump in.

I pounce outta my bed awash in sweat and vile tidings. Middle of the night. Can't swallow enough air, lubricated tongue plied to the roof of my mouth. Throw some water on my face. Some orange juice. Goddammit. Eventually…back to sleep.

Months later:

Ring ring.

"Hi. I'm trying to reach Gregg Turner."

"Yeah, that's me."

"Well, apparently there's been some clerical error. This is the graduate office at Claremont Graduate University. It appears somehow we miscalculated your total course credits for your doctoral degree. You're one course short, three credit units, of the amount you need to finish."

"What? That was eighteen years ago. I marched onstage, received my diploma."

"We apologize for the mistake, but your degree is no longer valid."

"What the hell am I supposed to do?"

"Well, the Dean of the College of Arts and Sciences has looked over your transcript, and she feels that to replace these lost credits, well, there's a lab we're offering on Dental Hygiene and Decay Prophylaxis—it's running now every weekend for a month. Apparently they need someone to be, uhh, *worked on*, extraction of a bicuspid. If you'd be willing to do this, lose a tooth, we'd rectify the error."

I am led to a reclining dental chair. Three hot babes strap my arms and legs down, pry my mouth open, and stuff gauze around my back teeth. I can't move, snug to the chair. The dentist ambles in, this older unshaven geezer in green scrubs. He's got a humongous toothbrush in his hands. Three feet long. He shoves the bristles in my mouth and scrubs my tongue. Not gently. The nurses, now suddenly looking horribly ancient and crusty, the leathery skin on their sneering faces now emulsified and waxy—they roar with laughter. They are toothless. They shove more cotton and gauze in my mouth as the dentist yanks out the brush. "It's time for the retractor, ladies," he announces. He produces large, rusty pliers and latches onto my top right front cuspid. CRRACKK. My jaw splinters from the trauma, blood streaming down my throat. I gag and he bellows: "PI IS IRRATIONAL, ASSHOLE—ha ha ha ha!!!!"

I launch out of bed in the middle of the night. Beads of sweat streaming down my cheeks. Sweating, sweating. Check teeth. Tooth still there. Washrag on my face. Gatorade. Gulp gulp. Goddammit. And eventually...back to sleep.

⇾•

Still, years later.

Ring ring ring.

"Hi. I'm trying to reach Gregg Turner."

"Yeah, that's me."

"Well, apparently there's been some clerical error. This is the graduate office at Claremont Graduate University. It appears somehow we miscalculated your total course credits for your doctoral degree. You're one course short, three credit units, of the amount you need to finish."

"What? That was twenty-two years ago. I marched onstage, received my diploma."

"We apologize for the mistake, but your degree is no longer valid."

"What the hell am I supposed to do NOW?"

"I spoke with your department chair. We think there's a way around this. You can make up the three credits—well, there's a cooking class that needs someone to sample the soufflé they are preparing for a retirement banquet honoring your dissertation supervisor.

This is happening next week. We've agreed to look the other way with the credits you are missing if you can participate—to sample the desserts with which they are experimenting."

I sit down at a long, long wooden table. Many prepared dishes: tuna casseroles, fettuccini with calamari, garlic prawns over couscous. Grilled salmon with "black sauce." They wheel out a tray of desserts. A chocolate soufflé is placed in front of me. This is our dark chocolate EARTHWORM *soufflé, they say. And they say it again. And once more. I look down and suddenly see small brown critters vigorously wriggling through the top chocolate layer. I am asked how badly I wish to complete my degree. It's a rhetorical question. This is a test, the final exam. Three spoonings of the stuff—I feel the horrid squiggling, the twisting and the turning—and the strong chocolate cannot camouflage the insidious concoction sliding down the back of my tongue. I gag, convulsing, digesting this snot-laden brew, and then I've lost all my clothes and then, naturally, my teeth.*

Bolt outta bed, the sun coming up now. The palpable olfactory shitstorm of the dark chocolate earthworm soufflé still too real, stamped on the smell sensors of my brain. I feel like vomiting. VOM-ing.

VOM?

Back in 1976, eight years prior to commencing graduate math studies, I was hanging with my hero, famed rock-write and author Richard Meltzer (*Aesthetics of Rock*, *Gulcher*, *LA is the Capital of Kansas*, plus lots of other wizardly beat-scripted lit). We were at the Variety Arts Center downtown in LA. The Weirdos, purveyors of crazy spastic "New Wave" RnR, were doin' their thang—alive on stage. Audience folks were bouncing up and down, "pogo"-ing, they called it back then (pre-mosh pit stuff—which came into being years later). We caught the fever and started hopping up and down sandwiched between tons of other folks doing the same. At some point, Richard spun to me and announced, "See, I can do it too!!" And he could! For real!

That epiphany gestated the embryo of the concept. There were Screamers and Weirdos and eventually some Germs and Bags and Flesh Eaters and Dogs and Pop and X and...well, Y not some VOM? We recruited another partner in crime, so-called "Metal" Mike Saunders—another rock-rit rick-rat (*Rolling Stone*, *Phonograph Record Magazine*) who specialized in heavy Stooges-wafted guitar riffing (and terrific Marc Bolan imitations) and hilarious song scriber in his own right ("Getting High with Steven Stills" is a neighborhood favorite). But you need some sorta song cred to get a big beat combo going and we turned to the Metal Man for the riff. Then Richard for the words:

> Electrocute your cock
> Electrocute your cock
> Lookin' for a hand job
> Stick it in a clock!
>
> Poke your sister's meat

Poke your sister's meat
Turn her upside down
And do her for an eat!

And before you could gasp "Lennon-McCartney," there were other top forty hits: "I Live with the Roaches," "Punkmobile," "Dare to Be Dumb," "God Save the Whales," "I'm in Love with Your Mom," and so forth.

Meltzer, now "Mr. VOM," and I traipsed down to the Rainbow Mealworm and Bait Company in the nether regions of the slums of LA lookin' for props. In a fever pitch, we frenetically gathered copious quantity of "Bronco" worms (they bucked up from the ground), roaches for the hit tune "I Live with the Roaches" (had to buy crickets 'cause roaches were considered "disease-carrying organisms"—not to be sold at a righteous bug emporiums such as this), and fresh-frozen sheep orbs (Mr. VOM penned the words to Blue Oyster Cult's "Harvester of Eyes," after all) and other assorted critter viscera. These were to be tossed out at unsuspecting audience folk watching live VOM do its thing. Throwing sheep eyeballs was a bitch 'cause they'd be tossed back at us and the joint would invariably smack of lamb. Just prior to the first chord being launched, in prep for our entrance, barbed wire would routinely be laced several feet high at the front of the stage and the "rhythm" guitar player (often *out* of rhythm and very *out* of tune) dumped piles of garbage and trash behind the barbs. That set the tone and the atonal tone was all downhill from there.

The first sighting of VOM occurred at this theoretically respectable venue in Redondo Beach, Kahuna's Bearded Clam. Honest. Mr. VOM, clad in a "GO VOM" torn-up tee, assumed lead singer duties (as much as anyone could actually "sing" these songs) and I, adorned in a "YOU ARE AN UGLY CRETIN" hacked-up black shirt, gyrated and pitched back and forth with the back and forth backup vokes. It got outta hand quickly. Crap started flyin' through the air, a creature and eyeball free-for-all. Metal Mike pounded on the skins (originally he riffed on guitar, but VOM-ette bass player "Gurl" had rejected his ZZ Top-like opus "Beaver Patrol" 'cause of offensive sexist-leaning lyrics (the line in the sand had to be drawn *somewhere*)—so he left the VOM reality briefly, but then returned as drummer). Some shit-brained train wreck who looked like Bozo the Clown started hurling burning candles from the tables and frantically pitching molten wax at us.

By the end of the festivities, Kahuna's Clam checked out more of a battleground than a music establishment, and the owner was super pissed, mainly 'cause all the hurled crickets were chirping (chirping, chirping) under the crevices of seats and tables—so we spent lots of time bug-ridding before eventually splitting in the wee hours.

This circus of live gigs persisted for just about a year, if you can believe. The capstone show was at the world-famous Whisky a Go Go opening for the Dickies. Stage wire in place, trashcans turned upside down and then the sonically foul cacophony just exploded! This time it all got crazy, crazy outta control—bronco worms, fresh frozen sheep's peepers (hurled out during our cover of "My Eyes Have Seen You"), crickets during "Roaches"—when the manager and sound guy popped a cerebral vessel halfway through the set. "That's *it*," he shrieked over the PA. "You're *outta here!*" The stage current was cut off. "GET OUT! TAKE ALL YOUR SHIT WITH YOU AND LEAVE. NOW! *I'm pulling the plug just like I did on that Morrison asshole ten years ago!*" Like, WOW! Rhythm guitar hatchet man was the last man standing onstage. He clenched his fist in the air and refused to go! But VOM was gone— and as the PA dude just bellowed with seething vibrations, the only other band evacuated mid-set from the place, gear tossed out on the sidewalk, was The Doors! A badge of honor. Or of *something...*

That was The End, my friends, we took it as far as it could go, everyone was exhausted, we'd had it. VOM sucked, but it was a gas while it lasted. Except, except—well, a couple of us we're having a hard time letting it go. Still armed with a chartbusting repertoire of catchy tunes, the Metal Man and I invariably hatched plans of picking up the pieces (entrails) and sorta maybe perhaps moving forward. Or backward. The distinction not clear.

Professional wrasslin' back in those days was unscripted and a wild ring hayride of fun (way before Vince McMahon ultimately morphed it into a ridiculous high-tech choreographed sissy circus and redneck costume show with the WWF). John "The Golden Greek" Tolos, perhaps the greatest of them all, routinely sent fans into a baited rage with despicable off-ring antics and locker-room interviews that were of questionable taste (hyping his upcoming world title match with Mexican folk hero Raoul Matta, Tolos looked into the camera devilishly and produced a big fat burrito from a paper bag and began strangling the beans out of it: "I EAT FETA CHEESE," he screamed, barely coherent with apoplectic fever. "This guy gums up his guts with THIS CRAP!!" And he stomped the burrito into a sad mess on the ground). Fast forward six months or so. Saunders and I were glued to the tube truly digesting this wrasslin' stuff one fine Saturday morning and who jumps into the ring? Why, it's the tag-team champs, the Wild Samoans! Affa and Sika. Wild, wild. But, Metal Mike observes, "too hospitable, not very ANGRY!"

Uh oh!

Ring ring...ring ring.

"Hi. I'm trying to reach Gregg Turner."

"Yeah, that's me."

"Well, apparently there's been some clerical error. This is the graduate office at Claremont Graduate University. It appears somehow we miscalculated your total course credits for your doctoral degree. You're one course short, three credit units, of the amount you need to finish."

"What? That was thirty years ago. I marched onstage, received my diploma."

"We apologize for the mistake, but your degree is no longer valid; you need to complete three more credits.

"What the hell? What am I supposed to do now?"

"Well, I've spoken with your dissertation supervisor and we've come to an understanding. There's a dentist in New York practicing... well, he needs subjects for experimental new radical root canal procedures...

Shit.

STRANGEST EVENT OF THE YEAR

Tolos shocks the wrestling world with 12 foot python

As publicity director for wrestling at the Olympic Auditorium in Los Angeles, I've had to really hustle when it came to promoting a big wrestling card. I never expected I'd ever be face to face with a 12-foot, saliva spitting Python.

It all began when John Tolos, the Golden Greek, came up to my office for a press interview about his big match with Freddie Blassie. Tolos had defeated Blassie in a rugged bout two weeks earlier. Now more than ever he was confident of victory.

After Tolos downgraded Blassie for turning soft and scientific to fans here on the West Coast he made a rather startling statement. "You fellows be at the Olympic tonight if you want a story. What I got for Blassie will make front page headlines." That night, two days before the big event, Mike LeBell was all set to interview Tolos for the TV audience.

As Mike called Tolos on camera he noticed that both big John and his sometime tag team partner, Les Roberts, were carrying a very heavy box. Tolos set the box down gently and told Roberts to leave, like a trained seal. LeBell asked what was in the box, but Tolos insisted it was none of his business. Later, Tolos went on to say that this was his secret weapon. As hard as he tried, Mike could not get Tolos to open the mysterious box. Tolos later told fans they would have to be at the Olympic and see the surprise for themselves.

Well, needless to say the Olympic was packed to the rafters on that warm night in September. Even I was puzzled about what Tolos had in the box. It would have made my publicity work a lot easier if I knew. I went down into the dressing room and all the way to the last door. Inside was John Tolos, reaching into the red box. As I entered he slammed the lid and asked what I wanted. I told him I wanted to know just what he had in the box. He looked at his watch and said in about a half hour you and all those other morons

will find out.

At 10:15 P.M. Blassie leaped into the ring first wearing the Americas' Championship Wrestling belt. The fans cheered loud and long for their new hero Blassie. He greeted them with kisses that only a matter of months ago would have been obscene gestures.

Then a strange hush fell over the crowd. Two Olympic seconds lugged the strange box while John Tolos carried a stretcher with a yellow stripe down the middle. The box was placed in the ring and the referee asked to see what was in the box. Make him open it", yelled the crowd. Blassie pointed to the large square box several times. Tolos just snickered and yelled, "This is your last match, Blassie".

Tolos then turned around to take off his jacket. At that moment Blassie ran over and lifted the lid of the box. For that split second a look of terror crossed Fred's face and sudden beads of sweat stood out on his forehead. Slowly Blassie backed away from the box. The blond backed into a corner, his heart pounding like a drum about to explode. He stood in his corner, motionless. Tolos, snickering with a sardonic smile on his lips, reached into the box and ever so slowly pulled out a HISSING, 12-FOOT, DEADLY PYTHON!

It coiled around Tolo's body, hissing and spitting. The crowd gasped in terror. My wife and I were sitting at ringside. She grabbed my coat sleeve and begged to leave. She wanted to get away from that ring as fast as she could. I imagined Blassie wanted to do the same. Referee Red Shoes Dugan leaped out of the ring. Fans at ringside panicked and fled for the exists. Tolos laughed and slowly headed for Blassie now almost paralyzed with fear. Fans screamed for Fred to give up the bout before the snake could reach and crush him. But if Fred gave up he would lose his title and Blassie just wasn't about to do that. Fred protested to get the snake

out of the ring. Tolos refused and finally uncoiled the slithering reptile and placed him on a corner ring post. Blassie grabbed Tolos and sent three punches to his skull. Tolos retreated to the corner where the snake was beginning to craw into the crowd. He grabbed the head, and as Blassie came toward the corner pointed the snake at Fred.

Blassie backed away. This went on several times. Everytime Tolos was in trouble he would run and get the snake. Finally Blassie sat in the middle of the ring. Promoter Mike LeBell came in and got both men's arguments. LeBell finally ordered Tolos to remove his friend or be disqualified. Tolos refused and the ref started a disqualification count on Tolos. The Golden Greek had no choice but to put the snake back into its home and wrestle.

Now Blassie tore into Tolos. The crowd went crazy. Blassie sank his fangs into Tolos' skull. Fred must have hit an artery because blood shot out of the wound in spurts. My wife who is not really a wrestling fan, will tell you the blood is real because a moment later they were fighting in the first row and blood went all over her dress, not to mention my suit.

Most of the bout was fought outside the ring. Blassie and Tolos both wore protective collars against one another knee drops. Tolos had Blassie beate several times, but the Santa Monica blonc wrote the book of dirty tactics and when Les Roberts, who was sitting at ringside tried to hit Fred with a chair Blassi ducked and Roberts clobbered his frien Tolos. That was all for the Golden Greek Tolos was counted out and Blass declared the winner.

When Tolos came to later that night he was not only mad at Roberts, but at th python as well. He stormed into Robert dressing room and proceeded to bawl hir out. Yet I never did see him argue wit that 12 foot Python. Come to think of it, wouldn't either!

APPENDIX A

TURNER'S PSYCHIATRIST CLAIMS "SONGWRITER DELUSIONAL SYNDROME" SHOULD NOT DISQUALIFY THE INTEGRITY OF THESE STORIES

I want to thank Gregg Turner for his bravery in providing me the rare honor of writing a blurb for a patient who has written a book. Did Woody Allen risk having his analyst opine on the roots of his pedophilia? Did Little Hans or Mahler request a blurb from Freud in the playbill? But Gregg is willing to risk psychological exposure in a heroic effort to expunge the demons that plague him. Most of my successful patients insist on a letter of protection as well as reminding me of the risks of a HIPPA violation ($10K fine and a year in jail) if I even intimate that I provide professional services to them. Not infrequently when I am a dinner guest, another guest or two will be my patient (Santa Fe is a small town), which stifles conversation, much to the consternation of the host. Speaking of stifling, I have to be uber cautious not to succumb to the urge to subtly signal my therapeutic relationship with the person seated next to me. "Here's to bestiality" would not be an appropriate toast to someone who had revealed to me their most shameful fantasy just the week before. So I thank Gregg for de-muzzling me and allowing me to expose him to the world. Well, actually, he has already done that with his music, and now this book. So let me try to explain a little about the author of this collection of obtuse observations.

To understand Gregg's writings one has to know his life history. He picked cotton as a child and now is the idol of millions. Whoops, wrong bio. He was raised in the bowels of middle class Los Angeles, the son of very nice parents. He had to claw his way out of this hellhole by becoming a renaissance rebel. He formed the punk band The Angry Samoans to provide a beacon for all those sickened by the pretentiousness of contemporary rock. A local boy made good, the Samoans took LA by drizzle. His lyrics encouraged his devotees to eviscerate an eye to demonstrate their existential angst. Wracked by fears of lawsuits if any of the impressionable teens who worshipped the band should actually act on his exhortations, Gregg grew timid and lost his edge. His life was becoming a riff on the classic MTV trajectory (musician struggles; has unanticipated success; falls apart due to drugs, egos, girlfriends, or hyperlipidemia; and after the requisite number of years, makes a surprise comeback with a wiser and humbler attitude). However, Gregg was determined to put his own spin on the obligatory Faustian path. He rebelled further and obtained a PhD in mathematics, demonstrating that he had no use for the physical or spiritual realms. Abstraction was the ultimate answer to the meaning of life! He would be happy differentiating indiscriminate functions for the rest of his mortal incarnation.

Gregg furthered his demise by moving to Santa Fe, a musical desert surrounded by real desert. There he fell into the grips of *songwriter delusional syndrome* (where the patient believes he is destined to become a commercially successful tunesmith) This severe illness is not to be confused with songwriter default disorder, a common condition suffered by millions of teens with guitars and too much time on their hands thanks to COVID-19. No, as documented in his infamous Kickstarter campaign to fund one of his delirious album projects, Gregg suffered from a profound and debilitating psychosis that failed to respond to a myriad of antipsychotics, mood stabilizers, and antidepressants. Benzodiazepines dampened the intense anxiety provoked by the failure of reality to approximate the belief that he had the capacity to succeed as a songwriter. To complicate his treatment, several professional musicians/singers recorded his songs. Like the old adage, "just because you are paranoid doesn't mean someone isn't out to get you," Gregg couldn't comprehend that "just because you record or sell a song doesn't mean you are a songwriter." For example, look at the Troggs. However, the sheer act of compiling this book has eliminated his songwriter delusion, proof that bibliotherapy can be effective even in the most severe cases.

Fortunately for the reader, prior to Gregg's descent into delusion, and later during moments of clarity, he wrote about the everyday strangeness of LA in the seventies and eighties and Santa Fe at any time. Herein lies true literary talent that bursts forth from a failed songwriter like... Sorry, couldn't think of an analogy. All I can say is that his observations of the foibles of his fellow humans are written with an immediacy that transports the reader to the exact time and place where reality becomes fractiously twisted and plausibly bizarre. What do ratings-obsessed disciples, world class mathematicians, and backwoods pest controllers have in common? Gregg Turner was there! And through his psychopharmacologically enhanced brain, he has managed to chronical their interactions with a unique and keen perspective.

As we know from the past four years, truth is stranger than fiction, and everything that is written on these pages is the whole truth...or something like it. Enjoy!

Jefferson K. Davis, MD

APPENDIX B

TURNER STUDENT JENNIFER STEPHENS BEARS WITNESS TO THE VERACITY OF STORIES

Gregg Turner tells the truth.

In the mid-eighties I was a teenage punk rocker in Seattle. Then I went off to college and was shocked and elated when I walked into my calculus class at Pitzer College and discovered my professor was Dr. Turner from the Angry Samoans. I got an A+ in the course (he said I was his best student ever—again, Gregg Turner tells the truth), but there were some crazy moments.

He would challenge our class when we weren't paying attention to his lectures and tell us stories about pus and tapeworms to engage us and get us back on track. Granted, it wasn't always back on a calculus track, but it was a true and entertaining one.

I was there when he tried to interview Hunter Thompson and told us about the crazy calls he got in the middle of the night. I told him that he should write down all of these amazing stories, and I am glad that he decided to follow through with this. These true and incredible stories deserve to be shared. Calculus with Dr. Turner was a very challenging and intellectual experience, but we also looked forward to the lighter side of the class with his life anecdotes. Derivatives and integrals were terrific—but how many college kids can say that their calculus professor was a true punk rocker with the stories to prove it?

Like the time he had the weasels and he couldn't leave his house for two days. Pure gold for my college years.

When I decided to go to NYU film school for a Masters in Cinema Studies, Dr. Turner wrote my reference letter. I got in. He has always been a steady and reliable mentor and teacher.

Jennifer Stephens, MA, Cinema Studies, MS,
Nonprofit Management